D0862369

**the power of kabbalah** for teens

Kabbalah Publishing is a registered DBA of
The Kabbalah Centre International, Inc.

For further information:

The Kabbalah Centre
155 E. 48th St., New York, NY 10017
1062 S. Robertson Blvd., Los Angeles, CA 90035

1.800.Kabbalah
www.kabbalah.com

First Edition
July 2008
Printed in Canada
ISBN10: 1-57189-576-0
ISBN13: 978-1-57189-576-9

Design: HL Design (Hyun Min Lee) www.hldesignco.com

100%

for tee

the power of
# kabbalah
Technology for the Soul™

# Yehuda Berg

www.kabbalah.com

**table of contents:**

**table of contents:**

To the people who make my life better each and every day: my parents, the Rav and Karen; my brother Michael; my wife Michal and our children.

# the path before you

This book has the power to revolutionize your life, the lives of your friends and family, and the lives of everyone everywhere. Yes, this is one powerful book, but the credit shouldn't go to me. The reason this book is so powerful is because it explains centuries-old wisdom that has radically changed the lives of many before you. But we'll get to that in just a moment.

The question I have to ask you is this: Are you ready to totally transform your life? I am suspecting you are, or you wouldn't have opened up a book on Kabbalah. Maybe you just sense that there is something more to life, but you don't know exactly what that more is. Either way you slice it, you're craving something different.

With that in mind, I offer you this one disclaimer: *The changes this book will inspire you to make will be challenging.* But as any good athlete knows, challenges can be fun. And if you carefully follow each of the steps that we'll discuss in the upcoming pages, your life will begin to unfold in ways you may never have imagined.

How does the prospect of endless possibilities and feeling totally in control of your life sound? If it sounds pretty good, then you picked up the right book. So keep on reading.

As you know, things are not always what they seem. Your best friend last year might have turned out to be your biggest headache this year, and that teacher who you thought would be the death of you (and your GPA) on the first day of school may, by the end of the semester, have turned out to be your favorite. Life is full of illusions.

There's one illusion, in particular, that often gets us into trouble— the feeling that there simply isn't enough good stuff to go around. *There's a limit to the happiness I can experience, the*

3

*wealth I can enjoy, the fun I can have,* you tell yourself. It's like being at a birthday party and watching the most exquisite-looking cake being sliced right before your eyes. Everyone is digging into a big, thick piece but you can't make your way to the front of the line. You start to feel uneasy as your mind begins to race with thoughts like, "I'm going to miss out. There's just not enough!" So you quickly come up with strategies to guarantee that you'll get your piece. Yet you can't help but notice that most of your plans involve keeping someone else from getting theirs. That's life, though—someone else has to miss out sometimes if you're going to get your just desserts. Right? Wrong. As you will see, it doesn't have to be that way.

Imagine the relief you'd feel if the host walked out of the kitchen carrying two more trays of warm, gooey cake fresh out of the oven and announced that there were several more on the way. You'd realize that there was more than enough cake for everybody. No need to expend all of that energy stressing over your slice—whether someone else would get it first. Now you can just relax and enjoy yourself, knowing there will always be more cake.

My mother not only understood this, but she *embraced* the notion of limitless giving, which made me one lucky kid. In fact, I could fill this book and several more with stories of the kindness she showed not just to my brother and me but to practically everyone she met.

When I was growing up, our family was considered eccentric, to say the least. My father and mother were studying a form of ancient wisdom called Kabbalah at a time when it was about as far from mainstream as you can get. But despite having few friends and little money, we lacked for nothing in our household. In fact, our stomachs and hearts were always full.

During my high school years I attended a yeshiva, or Hebrew school. This was a tough time for me, as I was often ridiculed for my parents' choices. In fact, the school asked me to leave before my final year: my family's decision to open up the secrets of Kabbalah to everyone was just too far outside of the norm.

Yet, curiously, the same kids who tormented or ignored me absolutely adored my mom. When she dropped me off at school in the morning or picked me up at night, kids would run over to her to say hello. If she was carrying bags or groceries, my class-mates would come lighten her load the moment they saw her.

How could they be so accepting of my mother, and so hateful toward me? After all, we held the same beliefs; it just didn't add up. I believe the answer is that my mom possessed something quite extraordinary—boundless love and compassion. People sensed it and were drawn toward it like moths to a flame.

Let me give you just a taste of what I'm talking about. I remem-ber one time my teammates and I were traveling to a basketball game at another school, and our van broke down in the middle of a snowstorm. I got to a phone (this was long before cell phones) and called my mother. Shortly afterward, she and a friend turned up, squeezed us all into two cars, and whisked us off to the game—in the midst of a snow storm, mind you—and we made it with time to spare! Honestly, neither my teammates nor I was surprised by her heroic efforts. She could always be counted on.

And it didn't stop there. When a boy from my school was diag-nosed with Hodgkin's disease, my mother sent hot meals to his house and arranged for volunteers to help care for him. You can imagine how grateful his parents were for the extra help and the kindness of my mother's gesture. During the course of his ill-ness, my mom and this boy became quite close. In fact, when he passed away, it was on her birthday. Just a coincidence? You could never convince my mother of that.

Another time, a ninth grader was hit by a car right in front of our school. His injuries didn't appear to be severe, but my mother, who happened to be waiting to pick us up, didn't hesitate for a second. She scooped him into her car along with my brother and me and dashed to the hospital. We all waited there for hours while he received stitches.

When my mother drove him home, she discovered that he lived with his guardian in a dilapidated apartment. That was all she needed to know before swinging into action. Although our own family had very little money, she hired two people to come over to fix up and clean their home.

That's how she operated. Somehow my mom managed to care for others, clothe us, and still make sure we ate well (even if it was only a simple meal of rice and beans). She never stopped to wonder what she might be giving up by spending her time or money improving someone else's life. She didn't seem to hear the words *can't* or *shouldn't*. I don't think those words were even in her vocabulary! She only knew how to give without reservation, and she gave knowing that her vast reservoir of love and energy would always be continually restored. Can you imagine living life in this way?

It's actually quite possible for each and every one of us. Now, I'm not saying that this level of love and selflessness is easy to achieve. We don't go to sleep one night and wake up saints the next morning. As with any skill it takes practice and desire—requirements that both of my parents were able to meet. When these stories took place, they had already been studying Kabbalah for many years. My mother had been working diligent-ly for quite some time on the very steps you are about to learn. She knew that in order to help others, she first had to learn to help herself. Only then could she offer her love without fear or hesitation.

It's like the oxygen masks on an airplane. We've all heard the flight attendants give the spiel about the importance of putting on our own oxygen mask before we help the child sitting next to us put on his or hers. Why are we reminded to do this? Isn't it a little selfish? Not at all, because without our own oxygen mask in place we may pass out before we ever get around to helping someone else. In which case we would be of no help to anyone! This rationale also works beyond the confines of a plane. If we aren't ensuring that our own physical, emotional, and spiritual needs are being met, how can we be of service to others? We can't. Pretty simple, isn't it? You'll soon see that the beauty of the wisdom in this book—the wisdom of Kabbalah—lies in its simplicity.

Not to mention that it has been tested by time. The principles contained in this book are older than any of the major religions practiced today. Actually, we have to go back more than 4000 years and to a man named Abraham to find the roots of Kabbalah. Abraham, the father of Judaism, Christianity, and Islam wrote *The Book of Formation*; and in this book he described the groundbreaking notion that we exist in two realms: one spiritual, the other physical.

We all know the physical realm quite well. In fact, most of our time is spent in this realm, agonizing over how we look, who we would like to date, how we're doing in school, and maybe over the drugs and alcohol we might feel pressured to use. The physical world is very much in our face, demanding our attention day in and day out. At times, it can seem inescapable.

But the physical aspect of life is not all there is—it just feels that way. Remember what I said earlier about things not always being what they seem? The physical world is the best example of this. Not only is reality more than just our physical world, our physical world is merely a tiny percentage of all that exists!

Some of you reading this might already be aware of this truth, or at least you've had an inkling of it. The rest of you might have to read the previous paragraph a couple of times to wrap your mind around this idea:

*There is more!*

But it doesn't really matter where you are on the scale of already knowing or just now realizing. Regardless, the path of transformation lies before you. And it all starts when we open our minds to the spiritual side of things. When we do this, we begin to see that acquiring something in the material world—a car, money, nice clothes, popularity, a boyfriend or girlfriend, the "perfect" body—fulfills us only for a limited time. The physical world may seem like all there is, but it is actually quite limited in what it can offer us.

It was Abraham who put into words this difference between the physical and the spiritual realms. This wisdom was passed down to Moses and then to Plato. Countless scientists, including Sir Isaac Newton, were students of Kabbalah—not to mention the psychiatrist Carl Jung and the quintessential playwright William Shakespeare. Yet throughout history the teachings of Kabbalah were kept a secret to the masses.

That is until the 20th century, when Rav Yehuda Ashlag deciphered Abraham's profound texts, making them accessible to anyone who desired a richer, more authentic life experience. Without Rav Ashlag, we would still be in the dark ages—believing only in a world with limited resources, chasing our tails desperately in order to get our share, and still coming up empty handed.

Rav Yehuda Brandwein was next in line to receive these teach-ings. He, in turn, passed them down to my father, Rav Berg. Each generation along the way suffered greatly for disseminating this invaluable wisdom, which organized religion viewed as a threat to its way of life. Rav Ashlag was beaten and left to die, while my father was ostracized by his community, leaving him barely able to support his young family.

But truth cannot be kept under wraps indefinitely. It shines through even the darkest shadows. Thanks to a new generation of teachers, today millions of people all over the globe have accessed and put to use in their own lives the incredible power of Kabbalah. You wouldn't be reading this book at this moment without their dedication to revealing this ancient wisdom. You'd probably be watching some clip on YouTube, downloading a song, playing a video game, or chatting with friends. And there is certainly nothing wrong with any of these things; they're fun. It's just that there is so much more for you to enjoy beyond the limits of the physical world. In fact, the energy you can "download" from the spiritual realm puts everything else to shame.

And you don't need a password. You don't need a user name. Actually, you don't even need a computer. What was once only available to great scholars is now yours for the taking—anytime, night or day.

Why were Kabbalah books and teachings withheld from the public for so many lifetimes? Because many feared that the principles might be abused if they fell into the wrong hands. How could something so inherently good be misused? Let me explain. Kabbalah teaches that the Bible actually contains a code—that the words and stories within its pages, although valuable in themselves, also contain another, more powerful layer of meaning. In other words, we're back to things not always being what they appear.

So even if no harm was intended, a student's lack of understanding of the more subtle textual meanings might lead him or her to misunderstand the essence of Kabbalah. It would be like my handing you the keys to a race car when you've never even driven the family sedan around the block. Without instruction you could easily lose control of a vehicle with so much power.

But what if I showed you the engine under the hood and explained how all of the parts worked in concert? What if I then sat you behind the wheel and explained how to properly engage the transmission, shift gears, and maneuver the car? In much the same way, modern scholars have discovered that given the proper education and support, even a layperson can learn to understand and utilize kabbalistic teachings. No longer must this life-changing knowledge be kept under lock and key.

But just like studying for a test, it's far better to take in the information gradually instead of trying to cram large amounts into your brain all at once. The same holds true for the information in this book. There might not be a test at the end—although the game of life comes awfully close—but still it's important to move through this book slowly and consider each step carefully. There's no hurry. Kabbalah has existed for countless decades, and its power will still be there when you reach the final page. Guaranteed.

Kabbalah isn't limited to people of a certain religion or ethnicity. Not at all. In fact, Kabbalah is the ultimate paradox—it's *custommade* for *everyone*. No matter the challenges you are facing right now or the difficulties of your past, Kabbalah is designed for you—for exactly where you are in your life right now.

And you don't have to sit for hours in a lotus position, travel to a remote mountaintop or take a sacred vow in order to access this wisdom. In fact, you'll grow the most if you simply try out some of these steps during the course of your everyday life. The transformation takes place inside you, so you can work on it while you're eating breakfast, taking a math test, or even arguing with your best friend.

At some stage along the way you have probably asked yourself some big questions about life: "What's the point? Why I am here?" You wouldn't be human if you hadn't. Kabbalah is a perfect fit for this line of questioning. It can help you to better understand your purpose here in this physical world, the reason for pain and suffering, and how the choices you make each and every moment can help you to achieve fulfillment—not only for yourself but for everyone around you.

As I said, you won't find a test at the end of this book—not even a glossary of terms to commit to memory—but there is one key word that you should know. That word is *Light*. What do you think of when you think of *Light*? Warmth, brilliance, and end to darkness maybe? Yes, it is all of these things, *and more*. Light is the unconditional love and compassion that flows from my mother. But it existed long before my mother—long before any of us were even here.

We have all experienced this warmth, this Light—even if it was only fleeting. Any moments in which you have felt genuinely happy, when you felt joy suddenly rise up within you—that's the Light at work in your soul. When you receive a compliment from a teacher or coach after a job well done, when you are giddy from falling in love, when you are laughing so hard with friends that you literally start to cry, when you watch someone you love earn something they deserve—according to Kabbalah, the source of this fulfillment is the Light. It feels absolutely amazing, right?

Why can't the Light shine all of the time? It does, actually. And we can experience it all of the time, too. But there are rules about how that works.

Look around. There's bound to be a light bulb somewhere nearby. Have you ever considered how a light bulb does its job? It seems pretty straightforward. You hit a switch, and light beams forth. But is the light bulb the actual source of the light? No, it simply houses its radiance. The real source is an electric generator located at some power plant, probably miles away. And just as lights don't turn on without someone flipping a switch, the same is true with the Light of Kabbalah. A certain amount of work is required on our end in order to experience spiritual Light in our lives.

And just as it is easy to confuse a light bulb with the light that shines from it, we often confuse a person or thing with God's Light. Have you ever fallen in love? If you have, you know how great it feels, and it becomes easy to fall into the trap of assuming that our girlfriend or boyfriend is the source of these marvelous feelings! But actually it doesn't work that way. *It's the way we act in relation to other people that brings the Light.* And that's what this book is all about—discovering that the Light starts with you. No one else can guarantee that you will feel its effects! And that's a very empowering thought.

If you want to feel alive; if you want to feel the power, abundance, and generosity that only the Light can give you, then you are in the right place. Think of this book as your well-lit path. Every time you open your heart, mind, and soul to the Light, you're taking a step closer to the home that's deep inside you.

# take kabbalah for a test drive, it sounds too good to be true

On paper I should have been just like the rest of my yeshiva classmates: we all came from Jewish families, lived in the same neighborhoods, and had the same teachers. But in reality I was worlds apart from my peers, which made for some pretty rough times in junior high and high school.

You see, my classmates were being raised in traditional Jewish families and were attending religious school because it was what their families expected of them. But most of them would rather have been playing than stuck in class with their noses in schoolbooks.

But I was different. I looked forward to school, even though most of my classmates made fun of me. I probably don't need to tell you that kids—especially unhappy ones—can be awfully cruel. But despite the daily teasing I wanted to go to school, and it was not because my parents made me. In fact, they never made me or my brother do anything!

Now, before you start thinking that we sat around all day watching television and eating potato chips, I should tell you that even though our parents allowed us to make our own decisions most of the time, our lives were quite disciplined. By grounding us in the wisdom of Kabbalah, my parents taught us that all choices have consequences and that we had to take responsibility for our own. This turned out to be life-changing for me, which I will discuss further in the following chapters.

What my parents taught us was not the doctrine that we were forced to abide by in school. Rather they imbued in my brother and me something deeper—a way of living that was infinitely more helpful than what any religion could offer. Religion usually embraces some sort of metaphysical or supernatural belief and includes a great deal of ritual, not to mention a lot of "right" and a lot of "wrong." With religion, you're expected to accept what you're told without knowing the why that lies behind it.

Religion is like being in school where all of the cool kids are carrying a certain brand of cell phone or digital music player. You don't know why this particular item has been designated as the "in" item to have this week; it all seems a bit random, but you can't help but buy into the theory that without this device you will never fit in or find happiness. When we buy into a theory like this, without questioning its validity, we are acting on blind faith, and blind faith is one thing that my father would not stand for.

When I was in school, cell phones didn't exist, but a particular brand of jeans was all the rage. When I begged my parents to buy me a pair, my dad pointed out that there were other brands and other types of pants available. Heck, I could even wear a skirt if I wanted to, he joked. My father was challenging me to consider what I really wanted to wear—and why—while helping me to see that I did have choices.

This process of getting to know what lies behind your desires is the first step. From there, you can learn to reshape these motivations into behavior that makes you feel good and is also beneficial to those around you. This is really what Kabbalah is all about. So even buying (or not buying) jeans can become a spiritual endeavor if you want it to be!

When I was in my early teens I looked at my peers—even the most popular ones—and all I could sense was the emptiness so many of them seemed to be feeling. Few of them seemed genuinely happy. They may have been wearing the "right" clothes and driving the "right" cars but they seemed to lack satisfaction and peace of mind, and it didn't stop there. Their parents didn't seem content either—and at that age, I thought that at least parents would have it all figured out! Little did I know. However, I did wonder how it was that the people around me seemed to be missing out on something that I had been seeing in my parents for years. Despite the difficult times my parents faced, they always had a thoughtful word, a helping hand, or even a joke to share. The Light was always shining in our home.

I was fourteen when my father began schooling us in Kabbalah. My parents must have sensed that it was time for my brother and me to start delving deeper into what fulfillment really meant. After dinner, we would begin our studies and would often go well into the night. I still burn the midnight oil to this day because of those late-night sessions I experienced as a kid!

It was during this time in my life that I remember making a conscious decision that I would apply myself fully to the steps laid out in Kabbalah—the ones I've included in this book. I saw that it wasn't wrong to want the trendy clothes or the fast cars or the cool friends, or even to have them. But to depend on them for my happiness no longer looked like the best way to approach life.

One of the things I loved about Kabbalah was that it didn't ask me to take any of its ideas on faith. Kabbalah says you should always test a new idea against your own experience. If it works for you, go with it. If it doesn't, try something else. This was a wonderfully refreshing notion, which made a lot of sense to me.

For years, I had been studying traditional Judaism at my yeshiva. Maybe your path has been similar—perhaps you have studied Judaism or have been raised in the Christian faith or another organized religion. Maybe this next part is also true for you: in my classes, I was taught to take the Bible at face value, to not question its anecdotes or commentary. As a student, I was rarely asked to test-drive its principles or the principles espoused by leaders at my school or in my community.

But when we believe every idea that is fed to us without investigating the facts personally, we are doing ourselves a huge disservice. The internet is a great example of this. How many times has someone you know forwarded you a story with a headline that reads something like, "Tiger in India Gives Birth to Litter of Piglets," or something equally absurd? Do you think to yourself, "Well, somebody wrote it, so it must be true," or do you check it out on another website? Hopefully, if you have been taught to question everything you read or hear, you'll do your research first before buying into anything and everything that lands in your inbox! You'll probably discover that there are elements of truth to many stories, but, like fancy cars and hip jeans, half-truths don't get us where we want to go.

It's easy to see that the internet is ripe with opportunity for misleading the public. But television and radio, newspapers and magazines, are really no different. We have been raised to believe that much of what we read, see, or hear in the media must be true simply because it made it to the air or radio waves. Did you know that when *The War of the Worlds*, a play by Orson Welles about invaders from Mars, was aired on national radio in 1938, people who tuned in thought the broadcast was the real deal? Terror gripped the country, causing pile-ups on the freeways and general chaos. People actually believed we were being attacked by aliens just because they heard it on a radio station. What was meant to be entertainment became a nightmare; talk about the power of media!

If we allow it, religion can have the same influence. Even though most religions hold *loving others as we love ourselves* at the core of their belief system, they practice this idea in different ways. And over time, many religions have chosen to impose lots of rules and regulations on their followers. As the rules piled on, the freedom followers had to question the established rituals and beliefs eroded. Religion became "should-based," instead of being based on a core belief in nurturing our natural desire to love and respect one another.

Think about it. When someone tells you that you *shouldn't* eat chocolate or you *shouldn't* play video games so much, how does it make you feel? You might think, "Why not?" or "Says who?" You might want to rebel. Or, if you buy into it, you might start feeling guilty every time you think about chocolate or playing your favorite game. One thing is for certain: Rarely if ever does the word *should* inspire you to act out of genuine desire. In fact, you mostly likely will never find true happiness if you just do things because you're *supposed* to.

The Light doesn't dwell in words like *should* and *supposed to*. The Light doesn't dwell in blind faith, either. But it does live in the desire to find truth and apply it to our lives. In other words, don't be afraid to collect information and form your own opinions. That's why we are here—to be information hunters so that we can find the truth, and gain certainty from it. Belief leaves room for doubt. Certainty, on the other hand, does not.

How do we become certain? We try ideas and suggestions out for ourselves. If your friend tells you that skydiving feels like floating through heaven, you can't be certain that's true for you until you jump out of an airplane. Meantime, you can choose to believe your friend, withhold judgment, or not believe your friend at all. After all, another friend may have told you that he felt totally nauseous when skydiving.

When your parents tell you not to stay up late because you'll be dead tired the next day, why do you think they are suggesting this? Because they've stayed up late before and felt like crap the next day themselves. Their hope is that they can spare you that feeling by encouraging you to hit the hay early. But you and I both know that until you yourself have checked it out, you can't be certain that you'll really pay a price for staying up until three in the morning playing video games or text messaging your friend.

This is not to say that we need to wear ourselves out with test drives. Your parents may warn you about not staying up late, and they may turn out to be telling the truth. Later on they may warn you not to gobble down endless bags of greasy chips because your face might break out. You may want to learn firsthand if this, too, is true. Over the years, though, your parents may develop a good enough track record so that when they warn you about the dangers of drugs, and of drinking and driving, you can trust their insight without putting it to the test. You could just take their advice, knowing they've proven themselves to be reliable. It is my hope that you will find another such reliable source in the teachings of Kabbalah.

We've all heard the phrase, "Listen to your gut." The reason this suggestion is so familiar is because so many people have tried it and found that it works. When do you listen to your gut? I'm guessing you might do this whenever you hear or read a new piece of information and you are not sure what to believe. Next time this happens, try it. Close your eyes, breathe in, and listen to your soft-spoken inner voice when it says, "Wow, I already knew this piece of information; deep inside I always felt this to be true." If you don't have this feeling—if something you've heard or read or seen doesn't fit with your firsthand experience—toss it out with the rest of the garbage. That includes what you read here in this book. We'll talk a little later about where this gut feeling comes from. For now, know that a gut feeling is your ally, one that you can turn to whenever you feel confused or overwhelmed.

- Happiness doesn't come from anything that you can buy, nor does it come from another person.

- You can't find lasting happiness by doing things simply because someone else told you to do them.

- To believe everything that you hear, see, or read at face value is to relinquish your power of choice.

- Religion and spirituality have different meanings. The former is usually identifiable by lots of rules and regulations; the latter is a life path designed to free you from "should" and "shouldn't."

- *Believing* is not the same as having *Certainty*. Only through personal experience and exploration can a person become certain.

- The reason we do not feel joy all of the time is because we haven't turned on the switch that will bring us the Light we desire.

- The tools you will need to make Light readily available to you can be found in this book.

Consider keeping a journal as you read this book, if for no other reason than because it's practical. At the end of each chapter you will find a set of exercises, and the journal will give you a place to complete your work.

But more important than practicality is the fact that you will be taking in a lot of new information. Doing some free writing in your journal after you have finished reading each chapter will help you process all of the thoughts that will inevitably start swirling in your mind. Were there points you passionately agreed with? Make note of these. How about points that confused you or that you disagreed with? Start a fresh page and make note of these, too. My hope is that these ideas will become clearer as you make your way through the book. You might want to discuss each chapter with a trusted friend or relative. If you do, however, pay careful attention to where your thoughts end and theirs begin. And don't forget to listen to your gut.

Finally, be patient with yourself and move at your own pace. Remember that great minds have spent lifetimes grasping this material, so don't expect to absorb it all overnight. Profound change takes time and dedication, whereas burnout gets you nowhere. There's no hurry.

Take a moment to think about your current beliefs. Why do you think you are here, in this life? What is the meaning of your existence? Be specific. And be honest—only by being truthful will this book be effective. Now, describe how you came to your basic beliefs. From whom or where did they come? How many of your beliefs have you personally tested to see whether or not they pass muster? How many of your beliefs came about because someone else convinced you that they were true? In your journal, write down the answers to these questions and any other insights you may have concerning your existing beliefs.

This exercise isn't designed to make you feel bad about why you believe what you believe. Just the opposite. The goal is to help you learn how to observe your mind and to simply notice whether or not your beliefs are coming from external sources or from internal knowing. Even if your entire belief system has been established by someone or something other than yourself, have no worries. That only means that you have lots of material with which to work and that your transformation will be all the more profound. No matter your particular situation, exciting stuff is on its way.

# it takes two:
# the 1 percent
# world of darkness
# versus
# the 99 percent
# realm of light

**L**ike Veruca Salt in *Willy Wonka & the Chocolate Factory,* we seem to go through life shouting, "I want it now!" But remember what happened to young Veruca when she finally got her hands on a golden egg? She fell down the chute for bad eggs, her indulgent daddy tumbling helplessly after her. Granted, Veruca is an extreme example of giving up moderation in an attempt to *have it all* right now. But we can all relate to when our need for *more* comes calling, its voice is loud, clear, and difficult to ignore.

Sure, some of us have learned a little discipline over time. In the Game of Life, we may have become better at recognizing that one square of Belgian chocolate trumps a whole bar of the cheap stuff every time. But even though we seem to be getting better at recognizing what we really want, those wants never seem to be fully satisfied. "There's always room for improvement," we think.

Our physical environment is a good example. We crawl into bed on a summer night and realize we are hot, so what do we do? We turn on the ceiling fan. With the ceiling fan on high, we start to get chilly; so we get up and grab a blanket from the closet. But now we notice that we need to use the bathroom. So, it's off to the bathroom we go…. You get the picture.

Similarly we want the "right" sneakers, or iPod, or cell phone. And after enough fuss, we get it. Ahhhh! Now, we're satisfied— for a couple of days, that is! In no time we are right back at the store, or looking on-line for the "right" accessory or the "perfect" ring tone. Our "needs" seem endless.

And it works the same way with friends. We long to be a part of the "cool" crowd. If we could only become friends with the right person, maybe we'd get a free pass to instant popularity. But even if our plan works, the results often leave us disappointed. First off, we might discover that our new friend isn't all that interesting, or doesn't enjoy the same things we do. Not long after that we realize our new friend hasn't made us feel any cooler than before. That's because *inside* we're still the same. That gnawing empty feeling hasn't dissipated in the slightest. We still want *more!*

Actually, our new friend might make us feel even more inferior; even more aware of things we're lacking. This particular brand of desire is painful because it never lets up. It is positively relentless. What kind of desire can hurt so bad? The desire for external gratification. And it belongs in what is called the 1 Percent Realm.

What do I mean by a realm? By definition a realm is a self-contained world. Your dreams are a realm, complete with their own characters, plots, and themes. If you are a writer or artist, you create realms everyday in the stories you describe and the artwork you create. Your thoughts make up another realm. You might be fantasizing in great detail about the iced drink from Starbuck's you plan to get after you're done studying, but that drink won't exist in your physical realm until you take action.

The physical realm is most familiar to us. It is the realm of sensory perception—everything that we can see, hear, taste, smell, and touch. Those we love the most are with us in this realm. So, too, are the people who we sometimes prefer didn't exist at all. The physical realm is tangible, touchable, and finite. Time and space call the shots here.

Our bodies are proof positive that the physical realm has its limits. We come into this world as fresh-faced babies. We grow up, we grow old, and then we die. Are our bodies that much different than a brand-new car that over time breaks down, gathers rust, and finally becomes irreparable? Not really. Since eventually everything in our 1 Percent Realm comes to an end, the possibility of infinite happiness—not to mention infinite life—simply doesn't exist here.

Another key component of the physical world is that when something happens, we react. This often leads to hurt feelings, pain, and ultimately chaos. In the world of the physical, every action triggers a reaction. (See, I did pay attention in science class!) But this goes far beyond Sir Isaac Newton's third law—this principle plays a fundamental role in our day-to-day lives. What do I mean? If every action has a consequence, then it becomes crucial to take a moment to think things through before reacting to any situation. Easier said than done, right? But with a little practice, this one principle can transform your life. Truly.

In fact, the purpose of this book is to help you to make conscious, informed decisions—ones based on certainty rather than on a reactive tendency. We'll discuss reactive behavior more thoroughly in Chapter Four, but until then, experiment with pausing—even if it's just for a breath—before you react to any uncomfortable situation. In this way, you'll begin to let a little more Light into your life. If you're still unsure of what this Light is all about, taking me up on this one suggestion will bring you closer to understanding what I mean.

We've talked a little about the limited physical world and the chaos that can dwell here. But we can't discuss the limitations of the physical world without acknowledging that a great deal of pleasure exists here, too. Dancing; trips to the beach; sexual exploration; staying up all night with friends; great new clothes, receiving an A on a paper that you worked on for weeks—the list of enjoyable moments seems endless. But that's the point—they are just moments. The feeling of pleasure comes, and then it goes. It is impermanent by its very nature. Try to think of an example of a pleasure that doesn't fade over time. It's impossible, right? Vacations don't last forever. Greatly anticipated prom nights come to an end. There will always be a last spoonful in that bowl of your favorite ice cream. Physical pleasures are not endless. However, there is a form of pleasure that is.

The real kind of pleasure that we seek comes from the Realm of the 99 Percent. And the pleasure that comes from this place even has a different name. It's called *fulfillment*. How do we connect to this realm? I'll start by explaining how we continually keep ourselves disconnected from it: by constantly looking for ways to satisfy our external, worldly wants. Which means that we connect to the 99 Percent Realm by doing the opposite: by turning our attention inward. Instead of seeking the next got-to-have-it gadget, person, or substance that will make us momentarily happy, we begin to look toward something deeper that will provide lasting nourishment. Instead of merely treating the symptoms of our discomfort, we begin to look at the root cause.

It's like treating a headache. When our head starts aching, what do we normally do? We reach for a Tylenol or an aspirin, right? We do this over and over again and our headaches become a fact of life, a chronic nuisance. But what if we asked ourselves, "Why do I have recurring headaches?" We might discover that we are chronically dehydrated or stressed, that we aren't eating often enough, or that maybe we have a deeper, underlying issue. But if we keep popping pain pills, we'll never discover what's behind our suffering. In the same way, if we continue to turn to immediate gratification to stave off feelings of unhappiness and discomfort, we are denying ourselves the opportunity for real joy.

My realization of what the 99 Percent Realm had to offer came in the form of a wool coat. Let me explain. As I've mentioned, my family didn't have much money while I was growing up, but the harsh New York winters didn't care about income and so warm outer clothing was an absolute necessity. After getting by for years with hand-me-downs, my parents saved up and bought matching dress coats for my brother and me. Yes, *matching* dress coats. Bear in mind that we weren't twins, nor were we five or six years old. We were in high school!

I will never forget the first time I laid eyes on that coat. I had such high hopes for what it would do for me—the confidence I would feel; the admiring looks I would get. So when I saw my new coat hanging there, I almost cried. Let me rephrase that: it was the 1 Percent percent part of my being that wanted to cry; that part of me that focused on what others would think; that part of me that wanted so badly for something in this physical world to "fix" me and make me whole.

I probably don't need to tell you how little I enjoyed wearing my coat to school, during a time when the kids my age were wearing hooded parkas and Mets jackets! No one—and I mean no one—was showing up at school in the kind of three-quarter-length wool coat that my brother and I were sporting. You can imagine what this did to our already low social standing.

But over time I developed a deep appreciation for that coat. How? I guess you could say that I gained some perspective. I came to realize how hard my parents had worked to buy it, and how much care and love they had put into selecting it. When they looked at me in it, they felt genuinely pleased. And eventually I realized that by putting so much energy into being embarrassed by my coat, I was wasting energy that could be channeled into the 99 Percent Realm.

Looking back, I see that my appreciation for that coat was a turning point for me. Without it, I would not have learned how to connect to the 99 Percent Realm, the realm of gratitude, unconditional love, and universal wisdom. This marked the beginning of my consciously allowing Light into my life. It also marked the beginning of my understanding that two worlds could exist simultaneously, with the 1 Percent World encompassing all experiences that have an end and the 99 Percent World encompassing the Light, which shines indefinitely.

Stop for a moment and consider what *unending* really means. It's hard to fathom really, yet it is precisely what we desire—fulfillment that goes on and on and on. We don't merely want to do well in our classes for half the semester; we want to *always* make A's. We'd rather not date someone we merely like; we want to be with the love of our life, *forever*. We don't want to be friends with someone for just a month; we want a friend that we can trust for a lifetime, no matter what. We want our desires to be understood and fulfilled, not just in this moment but continuously. And this *is* possible, but not in the limited world of the physical. It is a feature unique to the 99 Percent Realm.

Before you start thinking that you could never touch—never connect—with this realm, let me suggest that you already have. Think of the moment when you put the final touches on an assignment that you felt passionate about—one that took lots of time and thought to complete. That rush you felt was the Light of the 99 Percent. Or how about that time you took flowers to a classmate who had been injured in an accident or that Thanksgiving break when you did community service at a local shelter? That sense of purpose and peace you felt was also the Light. It can occur in any number of situations but you'll know it when you experience it, because you will feel peaceful and exhilarated at the same time.

Turning down drugs offered by particularly persuasive friends. Winning your first varsity soccer game. Making brownies with your grandmother one rainy Saturday afternoon. These are all aspects of the Light. So you *have* touched the Light. The trick now is figuring out how to get it whenever you want it—and how to make it last.

Earlier in this book, we talked about listening to your intuition. This is probably something that you already have experience doing. Have you ever had a feeling that if you joined a certain club, even though your schedule was pretty full, that something good was going to happen to you—and when you did, you met your future best friend, or were elected club president, or had a particularly fun time? Or have you ever had a sense that the boy who your sister was dating was not who he appeared to be, only to find out that he mistreated her in some way? This is your intuition guiding you. And your intuition comes courtesy of the Light.

Tapping into your intuition is like having someone pull back a curtain that has been keeping you in the dark about a particular situation. Suddenly, you are able to see it with total clarity. Well, according to Kabbalah, there really is a curtain, and it separates the 1 Percent Realm from the 99 Percent Realm. Of course, I'm not talking about a real curtain but rather a non-physical veil that keeps us from total fulfillment. Intuition is one way of pulling aside the curtain, but there are others, which we'll discuss in the pages to come.

If a curtain is what keeps us separate from our intuition, it is also what keeps us feeling disconnected from one another. On the other hand, *desire* is what brings us together. Whether it is our desire to protect the environment, to wage war, or to eat or have sex, we all have human desires. No matter how profound or trivial, these innate drives are our common link.

And if there is one desire we all have—it is the desire for happiness. No one longs for suffering. Not one individual on Earth would say, "Sign me up for pain and chaos. That sounds great!" Yet we often take someone else's search for happiness quite personally. Have you ever had a friend who suddenly seemed to pull away from you? If so, you probably spent hours reliving in your mind every recent moment you spent together, trying to figure out where things went wrong. Then, just when you think you've figured out how you've given offense, your friend calls to tell you that he or she has been sick with the flu for days and hasn't even had the energy to get out of bed. And all this time you had been thinking that you were to blame, when that wasn't the case at all!

Here's a true story that illustrates this point perfectly. I once knew a young woman who we'll call Sarah. On a boat trip, she ran into the sister of her very first boyfriend (let's call him Sam). The two women talked for a while, and before they parted ways, Sarah gave her number to Sam's sister, who said she would pass it on to Sam.

Sarah was thrilled that she might soon be in contact again with Sam. She had really cared for him during their relationship. Although they had parted on friendly terms, like many first loves, they lost touch. For the first few days after Sarah returned from her trip, her heart skipped a beat every time the phone rang. She couldn't help getting excited. But the weeks passed and the phone rang—but it was never Sam.

Sarah felt heartbroken. How could she not take personally Sam's failure to call? *I guess our relationship was only one-sided after all*, she thought. *All of those months that we were together must have been a lie.* The quality of Sarah's thoughts didn't improve, and she started to feel quite depressed about the whole thing.

Sam finally called—several months later. After an enjoyable conversation, he become quiet and then apologized for not having called sooner. He told Sarah that he had been suffering from a skin disorder and had been too embarrassed to call. He was afraid that they might arrange to get together and she wouldn't like what she saw. It was only then that Sarah was finally able to see the big picture—Sam's "avoidance" was about Sam; it had nothing to do with her—beyond Sam's desire to have her see him in a good light.

In the same way, when a person chooses a particular path toward happiness that doesn't necessarily mesh with our own path, we may get upset. We often take it personally, seeing it as some kind of reflection on us. But inevitably *it doesn't have anything to do with us.* When we take the actions of other people personally, we are allowing our ego to take charge. When the ego is at the helm, it will try relentlessly to convince us that we are the center of the universe and that everything we experience in our lives is about us. But this is a lie. Actually, our ego is the curtain I spoke of earlier, which separates us from the 99 Percent Realm, the world of infinite fulfillment. The more we can refuse to give the ego ownership of our thoughts, the more we can pull back the curtain to reveal Light.

This doesn't happen overnight, but it does happen. Things rarely happen all of a sudden, even though we use phrases to that effect all the time. "*The next thing I knew*, my car was in the ditch." "She *unexpectedly* broke up with him." "*Out of the blue* the coach kicked him off the team." "*Suddenly* my mom moved out." But is there really such a thing as *suddenly*? Do things really happen in an instant, or is there always more to the story?

For instance, have you ever awakened to suddenly find that your eight-week-old kitten was a full-grown cat; or to discover that you'd suddenly grown a mustache? Or that you suddenly lived in a different state? Probably not. This is because "suddenly" implies that anything could happen to us at any random moment. But the truth is, **things don't happen to us: we happen to ourselves.**

And in case you missed the significance of this—happening to ourselves is good news! Let me rephrase: it's the most significant piece of news you will hear in your lifetime! Why? Because if we are happening to ourselves, no one else is calling the shots. And while this means that we are wholly responsible for our thoughts, words, and actions, it also means that the possibilities for what we can enjoy in this life are limitless. Once we know this, we realize that we have already, perhaps unwittingly, shaped our past. But more importantly, we have the power, starting right now, to shape our present and our future!

When you're locked in the 1 Percent Realm, the world of the physical, you are a prisoner to reactive behavior and its consequence—chaos. In this realm life is a struggle, because you are constantly on the defensive. The words that come out of your mouth and the actions you take are rooted in fear and not love. As you and I both know, this mode is exhausting.

Thankfully, this is not the only way to live. When you are connected to the 99 Percent Realm, life ceases being an exhausting battle. That's because when you are in sync with the 99 Percent Realm, you realize that the choice between responding proactively or reactively is always yours. You are always in charge. Don't expect this to sink in completely now. The implications of this idea are far-reaching, and we will continue to explore this idea of *proactivity* as we go along.

For the moment, just remember that proactive behaviors (actions grounded in the 99 Percent Realm) offer the antidote to chaos. And who wouldn't want to be rid of chaos forever? In physics class you may have studied the chaos theory, or what's sometimes called the "butterfly effect." It goes something like this: A butterfly flapping its tiny wings in Tokyo can trigger a change in atmospheric pressure that contributes to a tornado forming over Kansas; a man slamming his car door in Budapest can set off a series of reactions that will lead to a cloud formation over the sunny beaches of Cozumel. The point being: everything is connected. Weather patterns only appear random to us because we can't track all the millions of influences that contribute to them—such as flapping wings and slamming doors. Today computers help us to see the ordered patterns in what appears to be chaos—*appear* being the key word here.

This is also true in our lives. Everything that happens has a specific cause, no matter how random events may seem. We tend to focus on the "symptoms," or the effects, without giving much thought to the underlying cause of the chaos we are experiencing.

The curtain—our ego—prevents us from seeing the cause. However, because the ego belongs to us, we have the ability to change it.

Before you were born, there was a time when people didn't make the connection between dumping toxic waste in the ocean and the thousands of people becoming seriously ill from eating the fish. The first outbreak of sickness seemed so sudden and so random; something over which we had no control. Needless to say, it was a scary time. But eventually, scientists made the connection between the toxic dumping, the fish, and the subsequent illnesses. Cleanup efforts began, and people got better. And once the relationship between Cause and Effect was made clear, the sense of chaos dissipated.

Everything is inherently connected, which means that your presence on this planet matters. Just like the gentle flapping of the butterfly's wings, your actions resonate much further than you ever imagined. And the more connected you are to the 99 Percent Realm, the more proactive and beneficial your actions will be. If you remain locked in the 1 Percent Realm, you will most certainly experience pleasure. But the important thing to remember is that the pleasures of the physical realm don't last. And they cannot be counted on to bring you lasting fulfillment—the kind of joy that satisfies over the long run.

That being said, Kabbalah isn't asking you to give up the worldly pleasures of first kisses, brand-name jeans, and long-awaited birthdays, but rather to think of them as little pick-me-ups that you can experience along your greater path. The underlying desire—the desire that we all have—is the one to heed. And that is our desire for the Light.

- Desire is our driving force.

- Two realms exist simultaneously: the 1 Percent Physical Realm, which by its nature only leaves us yearning for more, and the 99 Percent Spiritual Realm, which provides endless joy and happiness.

- Everything is connected, and nothing happens suddenly. There is always a cause. When we fail to take into account the interdependent nature of all things, we create chaos.

- We can address symptoms or Effects, but in order to make lasting change we must go to the root, or the Cause.

- Everyone longs to be happy; no one wants to suffer. Another person's path toward happiness, especially if it differs from our own, should not be viewed as a threat.

- Our ego is the curtain that separates the two realms from one another. When we remove the curtain, we gain immediate access to the Light.

- External desires are not bad, but they will not deliver long-term fulfillment in the form of the Light.

On a blank page of your journal, answer the following question: *What do you desire?* Don't filter or edit your thoughts. Let them flow, and write down whatever comes to mind, no matter how small or insignificant it may seem. Maybe you want to make the varsity track team, or bring your C up to a B in Algebra. Perhaps you want your older brother to stop picking on you, or you want to stop smoking or overeating. Do you want to get along with your parents better? Make a note. Would you like a car that doesn't die in the middle of intersections? That seems important! Be sure to write it all down.

Are you getting the hang of this? I hope so, because now I want you to write down next to each desire how you think you might feel if you attained it (fantastic, better, like a new person, more competent, etc.). How might your life change? (I'd attract more girls, I'd feel healthier, I'd be able to get a scholarship, etc.). Now consider what stands between you and attaining your desires. Why do you think you don't you have these things now? As always, there's no right and wrong here; you're simply trying to gain some insight into what you want out of life. Yet without knowing more about your true desires, you don't stand much chance of attaining them! So now is the time to be really honest with yourself. This information is just between you and your journal.

# the light has it all

**G**rowing up, my father used to tell me a traditional kabbalistic story about a kingdom in which all anyone ever did was complain. One man complained that he didn't have enough milk to feed his family, which didn't seem fair considering that his neighbor had enough for his wife and daughter to bathe in. Another man complained that his job required him to work twelve hours a day, while the fellow down the street only had to work nine. A woman complained that she was unable to sleep because her husband snored through the night, while the other wives had husbands that were quiet as mice. The King couldn't take the complaining any more, so he ordered everyone to gather in the town square and bring with them pencil and paper.

The townspeople were reluctant, but they obeyed. Those who arrived early sat on the few available benches, while the latecomers stood and glared at them enviously. It took the King several attempts to quiet his grumbling subjects, but when he finally had everyone's attention he instructed each person to fold his or her paper in two. On the right side, they were to make an honest list of everything they had, and on the left an equally honest list of all the things they lacked. After much rustling of paper, followed by murmurs and craning heads as people made sure everyone else was working on their list, the task was complete.

The King now instructed his subjects to go from person to person in search of a list that they found more appealing than their own. When they found one, they would be free to take it. But, the King explained, there was one catch. When they found a list preferable to their own, they had to take the entire list—both the good and the bad.

This didn't deter anyone. Upon hearing their King's instructions, his subjects raced toward the wealthiest man in the kingdom. His lands and herds were vast, and his magnificent home was staffed by countless servants. But a look at his list revealed that his son was dying of an incurable disease, and his wife no longer loved him. Not even the poorest person in the kingdom wanted a loveless marriage and a terminally ill child! So the crowd rushed to the next wealthiest man. But while his lands were also vast, he was unable to enjoy their abundance because of the bitterness he carried in his heart over the rape of his daughter. The father of the kingdom's next wealthiest man had gone mad and required constant care. The wealthiest man after that had lost his leg in an accident, and the one after that suffered from terrible depression.

And so it went, as people rushed around comparing their lists. The sun had set. Supper had been long forgotten. No one had gone home or fed the animals. Finally, the King strode majestically to the center of the square and asked how people felt about their lot in life now. As though waking from a long slumber, the people began to stir.

Not one person chose to exchange his or her list with another that day. In fact, by the day's end they clutched their own lists tightly as they returned home with a new appreciation for the lives they had been given. On that evening the curtain of the ego had been lifted, allowing each of the townspeople to experience the peace and joy that is the Light. With the Light in their hearts, they had nothing to complain about!

This is where that particular story ends, but it's not difficult to imagine that in a few days or weeks these same folks might come to forget the joy and gratitude that they experienced that night, and see everyone else's lot in life as easier, better, or more fulfilling. Once again envy would set in and complaining would ensue. So why is it so easy to forget what we've learned? Why can't we remember the joy and gratitude of the Light all of the time? The answer lies in the very nature of the 1 Percent Realm.

As we have learned, the 1 Percent Realm in which we spend most of our time is a world of Effects. The 99 Percent Realm, on the other hand, is a world where there is only Cause. And connecting with *Cause* is the key to transforming our lives. Remember the chronic headache we discussed earlier? Instead of being satisfied with taking a pain pill, we could investigate the situation further and discover that our headache is an Effect of a specific Cause. Maybe we are allergic to a certain type of food. Maybe we aren't drinking enough water. Maybe we need glasses. Maybe we've been consuming too much caffeine. Whatever the reason, there is a cause for our headache, just as there is a Cause for every Effect or symptom we experience in life. Remember, nothing is random. Nothing.

Think of it this way: If you remove a leaf from a tree, you haven't changed the tree. If you remove a branch from a tree, the tree is still unaffected. But if you can manipulate the genetic information inside the original seed, you can transform the entire tree—branches, leaves, fruit, and all. That is the power of the seed, of the Cause.

In the same way, the 99 Percent Realm is the DNA of our reality. Everything springs from here. It is the ultimate seed—the Cause of all Causes. The 99 Percent Realm is the lineage of all things. You might be thinking, *"This all sounds interesting, but how practical is this information?"* If you continue with the exercises in this book, you'll find that understanding the true meaning of *Cause* is incredibly practical. That's because when we understand that there is a Cause for everything, we stop treating just the symptoms. And when we start digging deeper, we allow real transformation to unfold.

So let's start digging.

If we set aside our material desires in life—those desires that are connected with the physical world—what do we find? What do we truly want? Do we really want a sporty car or do we desire the love and approval that we think we'll get from such a sweet ride?

Do we really want extra spending money, or do we want the financial security that additional income would bring us? Do we really want the cigarette or the alcohol, or do we crave the release that such a substance might momentarily bring us? The true desires of our heart cannot be weighed on a scale or held in our hands. At the root level of our souls, what we want more than anything are things like peace of mind, happiness, health, love, contentment, personal fulfillment, relief from fear and anxiety, freedom, control, and wisdom.

And only the Light can offer us these things.

I was fortunate. Although my high school years were challenging in many ways, I never felt empty or alone. I always had the unconditional love of my parents and my brother, so that even in my physical reality, where painful things sometimes happened, I lived connected to the Light every minute of every day. Sure, a nice car would have been—well—nice. And trendy clothes would have been cool. But they would not have taken the place of the happiness that my parents provided me. They couldn't have, because fast cars and happiness come from two totally different worlds.

My father describes disconnecting from the Light as being like the process of awakening from a wonderful dream. In our dream state, things are flowing seamlessly. We feel joy; life is grand, and we never want to leave. But waking up to our physical existence is like a splash of cold water in the face. When we disconnect from the 99 Percent Realm, we immediately begin to feel depressed, unfulfilled, or anxious. We want to reclaim those wonderful feelings we enjoyed so effortlessly, but in an instant we've forgotten how.

As with the townspeople from the kabbalistic story, when we disconnect from the Light we exchange gratitude for envy, and happiness for constant complaining. So long as we focus on all the things from the 1 Percent Realm we feel we lack, we will never be genuinely happy. But the minute we focus on all of the joy we have at our disposal, we plug into a state of being more real than any dream, a state of being that offers us far more joy and fulfillment than the physical world could possibly supply.

I could have been a carbon copy of the complaining townsperson had my relationship with my family not been a constant reminder of the 99 Percent Realm and the joy that was always available to me. To this day, I know that I might not have survived my teens—at least emotionally—had it not been for my family.

- The grass is NOT greener on the other side. We each have joys and challenges in our lives. Remember, if you are envious of another person it is only because you are not seeing his or her life in its entirety.

- Our true desires are intangible: love, peace, security, and kindness. These exist only in the 99 Percent Realm.

- Symptoms, or Effects, are part and parcel of the 1 Percent Realm. The 99 Realm, by contrast, contains the Cause. Only when we reveal the Cause can we transform.

- Connecting to the Light means making contact with unending joy; disconnecting from the Light means a loss of eternal joy and fulfillment.

In the previous chapter I asked you to write down those things you desired. If you want a new car, I asked you to write that down. If letting go of an addiction is what you want, I hope that you wrote that down, too. Now, I want to take this process one step further. I want you to look at why you want these things. Why do you want a car, a certain GPA, or a particular position on a team, in school, or among your friends? What are you really craving? Think about those intangible desires we talked about earlier (peace of mind, relief from fear or stress, love, approval, etc.). What do you *really* want? Close your eyes, and listen to your heart. Now, write down what comes to mind.

Take this list and compare it with the one you made in Chapter Two. In what ways are these lists of desires similar? In what ways are they different? Explore how your two sets of desires are pulling you in two potentially different directions. Which ones do you believe can be fulfilled by the 1 Percent Realm and which by the 99 Percent Realm? Mark each one accordingly. Make special note of any desire that appears on both lists. That is a great place to focus on as you continue through this book.

# your mission in life—should you choose to accept it—is spiritual transformation

**S**piritual transformation means one thing in Kabbalah: Learning to shed reactive behavior and to become a proactive being instead. What's the difference between being proactive and reactive? We touched on these important terms in the previous chapter, but now it's time to make these terms personal to your life. Only then, as you personalize these things, will you see what a large role reactivity plays in your daily existence.

How do you know when you're being reactive? For one thing, you will feel drained and stressed out. But you will also find yourself saying things like, "If my coach wasn't such a jerk, I would be playing varsity," which is like saying, *"My coach determines my level of skill and motivation."* Or you might be saying something like, "I can't afford the perfect dress to wear, and without the right dress I can't go to the dance." This is another way of saying, *"A dress has the power to determine my ability to enjoy life."* Or maybe you have found yourself thinking, "If I were skinnier, or had someone to date, or didn't have to study so hard, then things would be better." If so, this is the equivalent of saying, *If my external situation isn't exactly how I want it, then I can't be happy."*

Every time we use this sort of language, we are making someone or something more powerful than us. Every time we use this language, we are buying into utter nonsense! And it takes a toll—spiritually, emotionally, and physically. This is because when you live as though everything is happening to you, you must constantly be on the lookout for whatever life *suddenly* throws your way, and pray that you have the skills to make it through.

Reactive thoughts are generated *solely* by our ego, which is a highly untrustworthy source of information. The ego lies. The ego deceives. That's what it does. Why does it do this? To keep you and me separated from the love of the Light.

Another way to know that you are being reactive is by noticing whether you feel like a victim. *Why does he always do this to me? I try so hard and nothing ever seems to work out. Why do things like this always seem to happen to me?* If you are having thoughts like these, you are operating in *victim mode* and living under the illusion that everyone is out to get you. And this is not a fun way to live! When we go through life believing that the universe is working hard to undermine our every move, we give away both our power and our sanity. After that, what's really left?

By now you won't be surprised to hear that there is another way. And trust me, after playing the perpetually injured party, this way will feel like a breath of fresh air. In this alternative way of living, there are no victims. Nothing is happening *to* you. *You* are happening to life. You are no longer throwing up your hands in frustration at the random acts of unkindness that always seem to be heading your direction. Instead, you are taking charge and assuming responsibility for your every experience. In other words, you have ceased being reactive and are learning to become proactive.

Being proactive means recognizing that if you can't change a situation, you can choose to accept it. Being proactive means understanding that if people want too much of your energy or your time, you can choose to be assertive and establish appropriate boundaries. Being proactive means knowing that even though you might feel like screaming or cursing at a loved one, you can choose to act calmly instead. And these examples are meant to offer you just a taste of how becoming a proactive being can change your life. There are plenty more where they came from.

But for the moment, I would like to offer some perspective on how these concepts of *Cause* and *Effect*, *reactive* and *proactive* came to be. These words aren't just psychobabble. They are concepts rooted in the very beginning of time—in fact, they are embedded in an event that occurred before our concept of time even existed. If we were to travel back that far we would find ourselves in the presence of the Light, the infinite expression of God, whom kabbalists call the Creator. Imagine the Light stretching into infinity, expanding and giving of itself as it flows ever outward. That is and has always been its nature—to share unconditionally. The Light is:

> Infinite fulfillment;
> Boundless joy;
> Limitless enlightenment.

It is all of this and more. Unbelievable, isn't it? But have no doubt, the Light is real—more real than any pain you have felt, or than any sadness or anger you have experienced. Think of the greatest love you have ever known, your most significant accomplishment, your wildest fun, your best night's sleep, your most satisfying meal, or your most amazing kiss. Now, take these experiences and pump them up like giant, puffy cumulus clouds filling the summertime sky. Then make them larger still so that you can imagine them filling the universe and spilling over into universes that exist parallel to our own. When you do this, you're still only imagining a tiny fraction of what the Light has to offer.

This essence of infinite sharing that is the Light is known as the First Cause. In the beginning, however, there was nothing to receive this unimaginable gift. The Light flowed forth, but it was not contained, received, or enjoyed by another. In response to this absence, an entity was created to hold the Light. The creation of this receiver, the Vessel, was known as the First Effect, and it is considered the only true creation that has ever occurred.

It's important to note that because the Creator was the source of both the Light and the Vessel, they shared the same basic essence. Think of a cup carved out of ice into which water is being poured: the cup of ice is the Vessel and the water the

Light. In this example, both are composed of $H_2O$, so at a molecular level they are indistinguishable. They are one essence in two forms.

But unlike ice that melts and water that eventually dries up, the Light and the Vessel were infinite by their very nature. In other words, this wasn't your typical twelve-ounce drinking cup—not at all. As with the Light, the Vessel, this cosmic receiver, being fulfilled by the Light's endless goodness, could expand forever. Its entire reason for being was to receive, and it could do so indefinitely.

Actually, the Aramaic word *Kabbalah* means "to receive." The nature of the original Vessel, according to Kabbalah, was the *Desire to Receive*. Every desire that the Vessel had—and I mean *every* desire—the Light fulfilled instantaneously. Can you imagine such an existence? It would be like having an endless supply of genies and wishes! What a life! And, indeed, things were going quite splendidly for the Light and the Vessel. They were operating as one, a perfect harmony of sharing and receiving. It was impossible to tell where the Light ended and the Receiver began, like two lovers in an endless kiss.

This analogy of intertwined lovers is not far off the mark, since the two energies we're discussing—sharing and receiving—correspond to male and female. Earlier, I mentioned that according to Kabbalah, a code imbedded in the Bible allows us to read it on a deeper level. Well, here are our first two code words: Adam and Eve. Adam is the code word for universal male energy, and Eve is the code word for universal female energy. Masculine and feminine in this sense have little to do with the gender of the physical body in which we were born. They refer to the masculine and feminine energies that all of us contain, just as the Vessel itself contained both sharing and receiving qualities.

This Vessel was our root, our origin. Every being—all the souls of humanity, past, present, and future are contained within the original Vessel. And like the Vessel, we, too, enter the world as quintessential receivers. Think of a baby. All it knows how to do is to cry for what it wants, whether for food, a clean diaper, or a nap. Babies operate solely within the confines of *Desire to Receive*. But as they grow older and peel back layers of ego, they become aware that they also have another capacity, the *Desire to Share*. We are all in the process of discovering this essential spiritual truth.

So here's what happened to the original Vessel. One day the Vessel grew bored. Living in a state of constant receiving had lost its luster. Imagine having a credit card with an infinite limit and high-speed access to all of the best on-line shopping sites. You can buy anything you want with just one catch: The items you buy can only be for you—no gifts to friends or family members allowed. No sweat, right? For the first few days, you'd go crazy, buying everything you've ever wanted and having it shipped overnight straight to your door. Although exhilarating at first, by the third or fourth day you'd discover that buying stuff only for yourself has its limits, and that it would be just as much fun—if not even more so—to share with others. This is the situation in which the Vessel found itself. After having received the Light for so long, the Vessel had become increasingly like the Light; longing to share as the Light shared and act as the Light acted.

Before we go any further, let's talk about this word sharing. Sharing has many definitions, so let's run through a few ideas of what sharing might entail. Is it sharing when you loan your friend your car? Is it sharing when you tell your friend your deepest, darkest secret? Is it sharing when you give a classmate the answers to a math test? Is it sharing when you split your favorite candy bar? Is it sharing when you give away half of your least favorite candy bar? Are you sharing when you're having sex? Is giving a friend drugs an act of sharing? Think these questions through for a bit. Then come up with a working notion of what you really think sharing is.

So what did you come up with? What do you believe the key ingredients of sharing are? Let's go with the obvious component first. When you share, you give something to another person—something that is either emotional, mental, material, or physical. If this is all you have in your definition, that's okay. But what about when you're on the receiving end? Are you legitimately sharing the gift of another, or just doing something selfish—*taking* for your benefit alone? Kabbalah also gives us something to look for when we're trying to figure out whether, when we receive, we're involved in real sharing. That something is called Bread of Shame.

Although it might conjure up images of baked goods that didn't rise properly, you've probably guessed that Bread of Shame has nothing to do with failure in the kitchen. Bread of Shame is what we experience when everything is given to us and we haven't *earned* what we are receiving.

Reflect for a moment on your own life. I bet you can think of some examples that reflect this concept. Maybe you have to do chores around the house in order to earn money. Or perhaps your parents reward you somehow when you bring home a particularly good grade. In these examples, you are earning your "bread," and thus most likely feel no shame.

Or perhaps you find yourself on the opposite end of the spectrum. You do very little around the house, but your folks give you an allowance anyway. You buy DVDs, download songs, go to movies, and freely spend money you haven't earned. As a result, you may grow up believing that everything you want should be handed to you. The word "spoiled" is often used for children who are accustomed to receiving things they haven't worked for, and it's a particularly appropriate choice of words because their opportunity to experience the satisfaction of earning their own way has, quite literally, been spoiled for them. As a result, they may grow up feeling entitled, believing that everything should be simply handed to them. Until these individuals can lay to rest the chronic sense of "I deserve" they carry with them, they'll bear the constant burden of never having felt the fulfillment of earnership.

You can apply Bread of Shame to any aspect of your life. Think of how you've spent money that you earned yourself, as opposed to money that was given to you. I'm guessing you were a lot more deliberate and thoughtful about how you spent the money you earned.

Am I right? How would you feel when your friends complimented you on store-bought cookies you brought to a party, as compared to receiving compliments on cookies that you baked from scratch? Or, how would acceptance into a college based on your family legacy feel as opposed to being accepted purely based on your own efforts? Think about it. What about the feeling of being on a winning team that had few believers at the start of the season but fought its way to the top, as compared to playing on a team so loaded with talent that everyone expected it to prevail.

When we are the *Cause* of the happy moments in our life, we feel a deep sense of fulfillment. But when we are merely the *Effect* of someone else's actions, we experience Bread of Shame. It's that simple. Bread of Shame is simply a kabbalistic way of saying that there's no fulfillment here!

This is not to say that you should never accept another's generosity. Accepting generosity can be an act of sharing in and of itself. By accepting the kindness of another, you are helping that person reduce their Bread of Shame, which is good for all involved. But be sure you accept with appreciation and with awareness that the other person has something they need to share. For everything that we receive, we must make payment— the catch is that real payment is rarely monetary in nature.

For example, let's say your grandparents offer to pay for a year's worth of tuition so that you can attend a local community college. This is an offer you can't refuse, so you could just take the money and run—and feel Bread of Shame as an inevitable consequence. Or, you could accept the gift with the awareness that your grandmother and grandfather are not made of money. Most likely they had to pull money out of savings or cash in a CD to make this possible for you. They thought long and hard about this offer of assistance.

When you come from this second perspective, you can receive the gift and appreciate the full meaning of the check in your hand: your grandparents love you, and believe in you and more than anything they want to invest in your future. Your sincere appreciation of their gift becomes your payment; now you've earned it, and Bread of Shame becomes a non-issue.

Bread of Shame, however, did become an issue for the original Vessel. Because the Light was constantly sharing, the Vessel's existence involved no effort, no struggle. Eventually this didn't feel right to the Vessel. It got to the point where the Vessel became crystal clear about what it wanted: (1) to be the Cause of its own happiness; (2) to be the creator of its own fulfillment; (3) to share fulfillment with others; and (4) to control its own affairs.

And just as you would respond after FedEx showed up at your door for the fiftieth time with huge boxes from your endless on-line shopping spree, the Vessel screamed, "Stop, please stop! I can't take it any more." This was the state the Vessel was in when it resisted the flow of the Light of the Creator.

When I was a kid, I went to school with a boy whose parents had more money than some small countries. This family owned homes all over the globe. A chauffeur drove my classmate to and from school. A chef cooked his lunch. A tailor made his clothing. You get the picture—there was little the 1 Percent Realm had to offer that he didn't have.

But this boy was one of the most unhappy children I had ever met. His parents' money guaranteed him a kind of superficial popularity at school, but he was often moody and did poorly in school. Nothing seemed to matter to him, and he seemed to have no appreciation for all that he had been given.

It's probably no surprise that when his parents turned up at the occasional function, they behaved exactly the same way. They had inherited their money, and although they were impeccably dressed and looked the part of the perfect couple there was no affection between them; In fact, they barely spoke to one another.

On the other hand, another boy I knew from school didn't even have a dollar in his pocket. His father worked hard managing a grocery store where he had worked his way up from his first job as a bag boy. His mother was a receptionist at a local doctor's office. Together they did their best to give their child what he needed. His clothes were often shabby, but he never went cold. His lunches were meager, but he never went hungry. He took the bus to school or, during nice weather, he walked. As often as possible, his mother turned up to walk him home. When I saw his parents together, I noticed the respect they had for one another and the laughter and animated conversation they enjoyed together.

This family seemed to have very little of the 1 Percent Realm's creature comforts. But because they worked hard for what they had and appreciated the fruits of their labors, they had little Bread of Shame. In spirit, they were blessed with abundance and this carried over to their relationships and to the way they lived their lives.

I offer you these two contrasting examples not to demonstrate the greed of the wealthy and the righteousness of the poor—not at all. Money can be immensely beneficial when used thought-fully, and, most importantly, when it is used for the purpose of sharing. When we work hard for our money, we tend to spend it with more awareness and with a reverence for the infinite abundance from which it came.

Have you ever thought to yourself, *If I could only win the lottery?* Do you already have plans for all the things you'd do with that money? It might surprise you to know that most people who win the lottery end up losing it all within a matter of years. How can this be? It's simple: they had little respect for the money they hadn't earned. Unless a person truly appreciates the value of this financial windfall, this unexpected income can quickly lead to this individual's downfall! Without appreciation, there can be no joy.

So, how do we come by this sense of appreciation? How, once and for all, do we do away with this terrible Bread of Shame? The answer might sound a little out of the ordinary.

We RESIST.

You might be thinking, "Resist what?" Let's go back to the way things were before the birth of time, and I'll explain what I mean. We left off with the Vessel withdrawing from the Light. This is something we've all experienced—we've all pushed back at some point from that which gave us life. Justin, a teen who visits one of our Kabbalah Centres, told me one day that he had grown so tired of his mother walking him to school in the morning, out of her concern for his safety, that he'd started sneaking out of his bedroom window and down the fire escape in the mornings just so he could go to school on his own. Justin didn't feel good about his current strategy, but he recognized that his mother's protectiveness was inhibiting him from becoming his own Cause.

In the same way, the Vessel wanted to become the Cause of its experience, and, like a wise parent, the Light allowed this act of Resistance. When the Vessel resisted the Light, the Light withdrew and created a vacant space. This was an act of love, which was designed to give the Vessel the breathing room it needed to evolve its own divine nature (just as Justin's mother eventually let Justin walk to school by himself).

In this one ultimate act of Resistance, the infinite gave birth to the finite. The time and space that the Vessel's withdrawal created is the physical universe in which we currently find ourselves. In other words, the 1 Percent Realm was created so that the Vessel could rid itself of its Bread of Shame—the very thing Justin was trying to do by sneaking down the fire escape.

There was a second result of the Vessel's Resistance: the masculine and feminine energy of the original Vessel separated from each another. These two components shattered into countless pieces that scattered throughout the universe, comprising the vast cosmos and every iota of matter within it, from sub-atomic particles to zebras. This is how everything in existence came to have its own spark of the Light, its own life force.

Does this mean that even inanimate objects have souls? Sticks? Stones? Bones? Yes, yes, and yes. The only difference between the soul of a bone and the soul of an entire living body is the degree and intensity of their *Desire to Receive* the Light. Absolutely everything comes from the original Vessel, including you and me.

And thanks to the original Vessel's Resistance and the Light's allowing of this Resistance, we are now the Cause of our own joy. We get to put the pieces of the puzzle of life together for ourselves, instead of having the solution handed to us at all times. (What fun would that be?) In this way, we fulfill our deepest desire and our most basic need, which is this: to be the creators of our own happiness.

To help illustrate this, let's say it's your kid sister's birthday. You search high and low for the perfect gift and finally decide on a puzzle of New York, which is where she wants to live when she grows up and becomes a famous actress. The puzzle has already been completed—in fact, the pieces are glued into place—and the finished product has been framed. You think it will look great on the wall of her room so that she can see it every morning when she wakes up. Yet while this may be a thoughtful gift, how much fulfillment will a completed puzzle actually give your sister?

Now imagine giving her this same puzzle of New York, but with all 1000 pieces still jumbled up in the box. You tell your sister that part of the present is that once she's finished it, you will have it framed for her. She loves this idea and works diligently at it. It takes her nearly a month to complete, at the end of which you drive her to the store to pick out a frame. How much fulfillment does she have now? Do you see the difference? In the second scenario, you've given your sister what she really wanted in the first place: the joy and sense of accomplishment that comes from building the puzzle herself.

In the same way, we are here to discover this joy for ourselves. But the Creator knew that finding this fulfillment would have to be challenging; it would have to be worth our while. If not, then we would be back to where we started from—in the comfortable existence of the full-time Vessel, the around-the-clock receiver, the perpetual taker. So the Creator produced a series of ten curtains. Each curtain reduced the Light so that by the time the Light reached our physical world through the tenth and final curtain, near darkness prevailed.

Kabbalah informs us that these ten curtains create ten distinct dimensions, which in Hebrew are called the Ten *Sefirot* (pronounced "sefeerot"). At the precise moment of the Vessel's shattering, the Ten *Sefirot* contracted in preparation for the birth of our universe. Six of the dimensions folded into one, which became known as the Upper World. (Another piece of code: they are the source of the phrase "six days of Creation." Have you ever wondered why an all-powerful being needed six days to create what he could create faster than a sneeze? He didn't. The six days of Creation are code for the uniting of the six dimensions.) Of the remaining four, three are precursors to our three-dimensional universe, and the final one became the fourth dimension of space-time.

The creation of the curtains produced a series of dualities. On one side of the curtain we have reality, and on the other we have illusion. For example:

- If timelessness is the reality on one side of a curtain, the illusion of time is created on the other side.
- If there is perfect order on one side of the curtain, chaos exists on the other.
- If Cause and total fulfillment are on one side of the curtain, then Effect and lack of fulfillment are on the other side.

Have you figured out yet which side of the curtain we live in most of the time? You guessed it—the side of illusion. Fortunately, although the Light is dim on this side, it never truly goes away. It is still with us. If you cover a lamp with many layers of thin cloth, eventually the room will become dark. Yet the lamp is still shining as brightly as ever; the intensity of its light remains unchanged. This means that in order to see again, all we have to do is to remove each layer of cloth. But it's best to lift them slowly. We've all had the experience of walking from a dark movie theater into bright sunlight. If you're not prepared, it can be blinding. The goal of this book is to help you remove the veils and to prepare you for the presence of the Light.

If the story of how the universe came into being sounds vaguely familiar, it may be because you've learned about the Big Bang and superstring theory in physics. The similarities between the discoveries of modern science and the ancient teachings of Kabbalah may seem surprising, but the wisdom of Kabbalah has always been well ahead of its time. From a scientific perspective, the Big Bang might be described in the following way:

> Approximately 15 billion years ago, before the universe came into existence, there was nothing. No time. No space. The universe began in a single, infinitely dense point, known to physicists as a singularity. This point had no width. No depth. No length. When the Big Bang occurred, this singularity erupted in an explosion of unimaginable force, expanding like a bubble at the speed of light. The energy from this explosion eventually cooled and slowed, and in places it coalesced into matter—what we know as stars, galaxies, and planets.

Now, let's compare that with an excerpt from the writings of 16th-century Kabbalist Rav Isaac Luria:

> *The universe was created out of nothingness from a single point of light. This nothingness is called the Endless World. The Endless World was filled with infinite Light. The Light was then contracted to a single point, creating primordial space. Beyond this point nothing is known. Therefore, the point is called the beginning. After the contraction, the Endless World issued forth a ray of Light. This ray of Light then expanded rapidly. All matter emanated from that point.*

Pretty amazing, right? How about this description of superstring theory by the prominent scientist Brian Greene:

> *Just as the vibration patterns of a violin string give rise to different musical notes, the different vibration patterns of a fundamental string give rise to different masses and*

*force charges. String theory also requires extra space dimensions that must be curled up to a very small size to be consistent with our never having seen them.*

And the scientific evidence to support what kabbalists have known all along doesn't stop there. Physicist Dr. Michio Kaku, another leading proponent of superstring theory, wrote the following:

*The Universe is a symphony of vibrating strings. And when strings move in ten-dimensional space-time, they warp the space-time surrounding them in precisely the way predicted by general relativity. Physicists retrieve our more familiar four-dimensional universe by assuming that, during the Big Bang, six of the ten dimensions curled up into a tiny ball, while the remaining four expanded explosively, giving us the Universe we see.*

It's no coincidence that the number of dimensions required to make the theory work (ten) and the number of dimensions condensed into one (six) is identical to the numbers given by the ancient kabbalists. Science is finally starting to reveal what has existed on the other side of the curtain all along—an entire realm that our limited physical senses have completely overlooked!

With this in mind, let's return to the Vessel, which took a very proactive step when it decided to become its own Cause. After feeling like a victim of a condition that nowadays affects many kids, I also had to figure out what it meant to become my own cause at an early age. I owe this to ADD, or Attention Deficit Disorder, something that has been a part of my life for as long as I can remember. Even now, after fifteen minutes or so, my attention span is shot. If I'm sitting, I need to stand up and walk around. If I'm walking around, I usually decide to make a phone call or multi-task in some way while I'm at it. At the office, I have various knickknacks on my desk to occupy my hands while I work.

As an adult, I have learned how to work around my tendency to be distracted. But as a kid, my lack of focus proved to be quite a challenge. Not only did I have trouble paying attention during class, but one of the side effects was that I felt disconnected from everything and everyone. It was just another way in which I didn't fit in.

On the very first day of kindergarten, I remember standing outside at the playground with my father. As I held his hand tight, I watched all the other kids goof around and have fun. They weren't playing with *me,* and I couldn't figure out why. Needless to say, this is not one of my favorite childhood memories. But what I realized later was that all I needed to do was walk over and play with them! My classmates were already in the midst of play, already engaged in fun. I was waiting for them to "happen" to me rather than being proactive and introducing myself to them.

The concept of children at play is actually a pretty good analogy for the interaction that exists between the Light and us. At one time or another, we have all stood on the outside of joy and fulfillment, wondering why it isn't coming our way, when all along the enjoyment (the Light) was ours for the taking.

My parents and teachers worked hard to help me with my ADD, and I was appreciative of their efforts. But it wasn't until I started to take responsibility for my own circumstances that I began to see real change unfold in my life. My attempts were admittedly forced in the beginning. I literally made myself start conversations with classmates even though I was freaking out inside. It wasn't that I was shy; I was completely disconnected from my surroundings, so forging a bond with anyone besides my immediate family seemed totally unfamiliar to me. Most of the time, the kids I talked to had no clue of the fear I felt. Either way, in the beginning it wasn't about them— it was about healing myself. That's where I had to start.

As I kid with ADD, I sometimes skipped class. Without the ability to focus, I simply couldn't learn in a classroom environment. Instead, I would go for long walks and think about the principles of Kabbalah that my father was teaching me at home. I began to use those lessons to challenge my sense that life was happening to me. With this fundamental change in perspective, I started to reshape my circumstances into a life that I enjoyed, and could be proud of.

Sure, I struggled with ADD (as well as dyslexia), but everyone carries a thorn of some sort in one's side—and many of these thorns are far more painful than what I was dealing with. As I looked around me, I saw plenty of kids who might not have had my learning disabilities, but who came from broken or unhappy families, or had other challenges to overcome. Sure, my life would have been easier without my disorders, but would it have been better? I don't think so.

If there was a practical benefit of having ADD it was that it kept me out of trouble. Since most of my schoolmates wrote me off as weird and introverted, I usually wasn't the first person they thought of when someone's parents went away for the weekend and didn't lock the liquor cabinet, or when there was a late night party on the outskirts of town. In retrospect, I can see how my ADD actually helped keep me safe.

That being said, there's always a reason, or cause, for the circumstances that we experience in our lives—always. Someone who is overweight as a teenager may feel lonely, frustrated, and depressed. *Why me?* They may think. *Why can't I have a normal body like everyone else?* Yet their excess weight may have saved them from a painful experience. It may have kept them from having casual sex that might have resulted in an unwanted pregnancy or a sexually transmitted disease. These would have been far worse than carrying an extra 20 pounds, although at the time, nothing could have felt worse than not being at a "normal" weight.

In the same way, my ADD served a purpose. At first, my ADD was all about teaching me to overcome the insecurity and discomfort that I felt. But eventually it taught me how I could share with others the joy that I was receiving. The more I was able to transform my struggles into positive energy, the more energy I could impart to people who were struggling through painful situations of their own. Only through sharing are we able to experience the Light of the Creator for ourselves, as well as reveal it to others. In fact, sharing is one of the Light's key attributes that we must express in our physical world in order to remove Bread of Shame. The good news is that because we are made of the Light, we already contain the *Desire to Share* within our DNA.

In addition to sharing, here are the other three attributes that are required for proactive living:

- Being the Cause;
- Being a Creator;
- Being in Control.

We could call them the 3 Cs. Through these attributes, the Light makes it clear that the world is not something that just happens to us. It is something we make happen every second of every day.

Conversely, the traits of the Vessel are reactive:

- Being the Effect;
- Being a Created Entity;
- Being Under the Control of Everything;
- Receiving.

Reactive behavior includes anger, envy, resentment, low self-esteem, greed, and dishonesty. The reality is that 99 Percent of our behavior is reactive. So what can you do about it? Become the cause, take control of your life, and share the Light you have within you! If it sounds like too much to handle, have no worries. The newness of these concepts will wear off, but their transformative power will remain forever. Hang in there and you'll see firsthand how these principles can be applied to your world—with truly awesome effects!

- If life feels as if it is happening to you or that you are merely the Effect, or victim, of someone else's behavior, then you are being reactive.

- When you are the Cause of whatever is happening, you are being proactive.

- The Light of the Creator existed before time. Its essence of infinite sharing, also called the *Desire to Share*, is known as the First Cause.

- The Creator created The Vessel so that The Vessel could receive the gift of its Light. This is known as the First Effect. The basic nature of the Vessel is the *Desire to Receive*.

- The union of the Vessel and the Light created the Endless World.

- Because the Vessel came from the Creator, it had within it the *Desire to Receive*, as well as the *Desire to Share*.

- Bread of Shame occurs when you receive something without having earned it.

- In order to rid itself of Bread of Shame, the Vessel resisted the Light. This single act created the 1 Percent Realm, which is home to the cosmos and everything in it, including you and me.

- We all contain an aspect of the Light.

- Ten curtains (*Sefirot*) were created to separate the 1 Percent Realm from the Light. During the Vessel's Resistance, six of these folded into one.

- Current Big Bang and superstring theories are markedly similar to kabbalistic beliefs regarding the creation of the universe.

- Taking responsibility for your life circumstances is the first step of proactive behavior.

- The *Desire to Share* is already within us, but it's up to each of us to activate it.

Make a list of all the times that your parents, teachers, relatives, and friends have tried to help you out with a problem or situation. Now consider how those times made you feel. Did they make you feel cared for and nurtured? Did any of these moments make you wish that the person had left you alone to take care of the problem yourself? Did any of these situations make you feel as if you couldn't do things on your own, or as if you were the Effect of decisions and choices rather than the Cause of your own experience? Did the actions of the other person in any way undermine your ability to care for yourself? In what way could the situation have been more enjoyable or beneficial? Do any of these include taking a more active role in your own success or happiness? Think about each incidence carefully, and write down your thoughts.

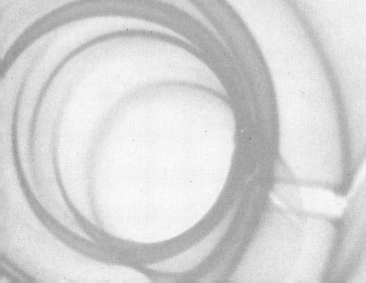

# moments of transformation are direct links with the 99 percent realm

**W**hen I was growing up, nothing beat watching the New York Knicks play basketball. Seeing Patrick Ewing and Mark Jackson use their skills to double-team their opponents probably brought me as much of an adrenaline rush as it did them. Most of the time my brother and I were relegated to watching the excitement on television, but once in a blue moon we'd be given tickets to go see the real thing. It was pure magic!

Actually, it was my team's nemesis, Michael Jordan of the Chicago Bulls, who first taught me about transformation. Watching him as he moved across the court, it was hard to deny that this was a man who knew how to connect with the 99 Percent Realm—again and again. He seemed to defy the physical laws of this planet as he hung in the air, breaking record after record. I've never seen a human being move the way he did. And much as it pained me to see him use his magic against my home team, I was absolutely mesmerized by his talents.

Simply put, I wanted what Michael Jordan had—not necessarily to be the best basketball player on the planet but to be plugged into the 99 Percent Realm the way he was. At the time, I don't think I really believed it was possible. After all, I was an outsider with no one on my home court but my family and Kabbalah. But the older I grew, the more I realized that these two things were all I needed to transform my life into something every bit as extraordinary and miraculous as the life Michael Jordan seemed to be living.

Believe it or not, before every decision we make there exists a millisecond when all things are possible. Better still, we can train our minds to use this moment to our advantage. How? By choosing—in this one small sliver of time—to act based on the *Desire to Share* (which is proactive) rather than the *Desire to Receive* (which is reactive). Every time we do this, every time we resist a knee-jerk reaction, we transform a particular aspect of ourselves. When Michael Jordan was on the court I'm sure he was aware of everyone else's actions, yet he usually chose not to respond to them. Rather, he implemented and executed his own strategy, and by being proactive in this way he elevated his own game as well as that of his entire team.

We might not be professional basketball players, but like Michael Jordan we have the choice every second of every day to either be the Cause of our joy or the Effect of external events. We get a C on a test, so we talk trash about the teacher. We hear a rumor about a classmate, and we pass the gossip along to another classmate. Event, reaction; event, reaction. On and on it goes. But we don't have to live like this. We can become creators instead of reactors. We can become the Cause. And when we become the Cause we are no longer swayed by outside forces, positive or negative. We have gained control. We're no longer helpless, and who wouldn't want that?

According to Kabbalah, having control isn't the way it appears in some comic book. When we have control, we don't rule the world or control the weather. Having control means we have the power to choose to share. When we forget or refuse to share— when we rely solely on receiving—we are pleasing only our ego; consciously or not, we are living our lives in darkness. Our ego thrives on reactive behavior because, reacting to something, we are all about "me"—which is what keeps us from the Light.

Let me be clear here; when I say ego, I'm not talking about a healthy sense of self—the part of you that takes pleasure in being praised for a dinner that you prepared well, or the satis- faction you get in seeing a website you designed on the internet, or in standing up to the bully who's been teasing your kid sister. I'm talking about the ego that thinks that whenever it rains, it's wrecking *your* day (even though it's raining on the entire city). Or if your brother doesn't want to help you with your homework, it's because he doesn't care about you—not because he might have had a crummy day at school. This is the ego I'm referring to—the one that leads us to believe that we are the center of the universe.

All too often our ego leads us to interpret the actions of others as "anti-me," whereas in reality their actions have nothing to do with us. When we learn not to take things so personally, we're free to be much happier. Think about it: If there is a bad storm system moving over your city, you are not the only one affected. The entire city now has to negotiate the slippery roads and reschedule appointments. If your mom and dad have asked you to babysit your little sister on Friday night so that they can have a night to themselves, this may seem terribly unfair; after all, you already had tentative plans that night to hang out with your friends. But what about all of the times that your parents have let you go out and enjoy yourself? Wouldn't it make sense that they might want to do the same sometimes?

A few years ago a scientific study revealed that people who frequently used the words *me*, *my*, and *mine* suffered from heart attacks more often than their less self-centered counterparts. It sounds like their hearts were too caught up in ego instead of opening and sharing!

It's easy to get caught up in ego. After all, the ego expects to receive what it wants when it wants it. It also likes being the center of attention! But we can counter these tendencies by learning to resist our ego. Give it a try and see what happens. But start small. Resisting the ego is trickier than it sounds. Remember that the ego is the most deceptive and manipulative part of yourself, that it's willing to use every trick in the book to steer you off course and away from the Light.

Katie had been coming to one of our Kabbalah Centres for years, and one day she shared with me a painful story about resisting her ego. Katie lived with her mother and her mother's boyfriend, Daniel. Daniel used to beat Katie's mother regularly, but her mother refused to leave him. Despite the continued abuse, Katie said, her mother kept hoping that over time her love could change Daniel. As you might have guessed, Daniel wasn't terribly interested in changing.

One day Katie came home from school to find her mom lying on the kitchen floor unconscious, and covered in blood. At first, Katie thought her mother was dead. At the hospital the doctors told Katie that her mother had a broken arm, two broken legs, a crushed rib, and head injuries. The doctors couldn't tell Katie whether or not her mom would fully recover. They would just have to wait and see.

Katie was overcome with grief and anger. In her fury, she remembered that her father had given her mom a gun for protection years ago, and Katie knew just where her mother kept it. So Katie loaded the gun and went out looking for Daniel. Sure enough, she found him outside his favorite bar, flirting with a woman. Katie hid behind a nearby tree.

"He was just a few feet away," Katie told me. "I could have shot him so easily, and I felt completely justified in doing so." But despite her sense of justification, Katie didn't act. She had been taking Kabbalah classes, and what she had been learning popped into her mind. With the gun still in her hand, she took a breath and forced herself to pause. In that moment she realized that by standing there with the gun aimed at Daniel—however powerful she might feel, even though she could be the Cause of his pain, her actions were the Effect of his—she would be giving her power away. She was merely the effect, and he was the cause. And as soon as she realized this, she lowered the gun and returned to the hospital to be with her mom. In the moment Katie decided not to use the gun, she became the Cause, thereby revealing Light to herself and to the world.

Reacting is the easy route. And because it's easy, it results in Bread of Shame, which is exactly the opposite of what we are striving for. Whether we react passively or aggressively, it makes no difference. As long as we slip into our natural reactive tendency in any given situation, we are relinquishing our free choice. Within the 1 Percent Realm, our free choice consists solely of being reactive or being proactive. This might not seem like such a huge choice, but what you decide can make the difference between joy and sadness, Light and darkness, life and death.

If you're like me, you may think that most aspects of your life involve free choice: You can eat a big juicy steak or a veggie burger; you can drink a Coke or a glass of water; you can study for a test or watch television, and so on. But in each case, you are not making a choice at all; you are simply satisfying a desire, which means that you are an effect in all of these situations. Whether you eat a steak or go for the veggie burger isn't the point. You are merely acting as an Effect caused by your hunger. Free choice comes into play when you choose to restrict that hunger or desire—or when you *choose* not to.

When we react to something, we are tapping into our primitive nature. We are acting in the same way that a wild animal acts. Its desires and reactions are purely impulsive; if you have ever watched National Geographic videos in science class, you know that instant gratification is the name of the game in the animal kingdom. But we aren't animals (although we might act like it sometimes). We have the ability to pause first and choose to restrict our response. When we do this, we are tapping into our God nature, the part of our nature that we received from the Light in the very beginning. By connecting with our God-given nature, we are choosing to be the Cause of our desire, and no longer merely its Effect. Restriction, by the way, doesn't mean that we won't decide to satiate that desire after all. It just means that we pause and make a conscious decision. Our ability to act with awareness is what makes us human.

Let's say you are waiting for your date to pick you up at your house. You're wearing your favorite dress or your favorite khakis and shirt, and you look good. You're excited about the evening, but as the hand on the clock passes the anticipated hour and your date has not yet arrived, disappointment sets in. Your cell phone rings. It's your date calling to cancel. How do you respond?

You might put on some comfy clothes and treat yourself to a pint of Ben and Jerry's as a form of self-therapy. Or you could hop in your car, drive over to your date's house, and chew him or her out. Or you could call up everyone you know and tell them what a rotten person your date turned out to be. These are all things you could do, but do you see that each of these responses is a reaction to the phone call, because all of them are coming from a place of anger and resentment? What if you were to say to yourself instead, "If my date cancelled, perhaps it was for a good reason. And if it wasn't, then I'm delighted that they've saved me from wasting a minute more of my time in that relationship." By being proactive in this way, we are resisting our knee-jerk reaction to an event or a series of events. The more effectively we are able to resist, the more we open ourselves to the Light.

If we are truly honest, we should acknowledge that one of the main reasons we react to things is because it fuels us with instant gratification. Blowing off steam feels very satisfying in the moment. Reacting manipulatively makes us feel as though we are in control. Responding with a false laugh or smile makes people like us in that moment. But such responses only offer us temporary glimpses of the 99 Percent Realm. Not to mention that when our desires are immediately gratified, more often than not we experience Bread of Shame. But even these momentary connections with the 99 Percent Realm give us a hint of the potential of the Light's profound transformative power. The only way to hold onto that magic, however, is to resist our reactive behavior on a consistent basis.

So the most challenging part about reacting is the good feeling that it can give us, even though it's not good for us in the long run. When someone compliments us on a new outfit or a new hairstyle, this can make us feel great—but in these examples the other person is the Cause of our good feelings and we are merely the Effect. Because of this, our sense of pleasure will only be temporary and we run the risk of becoming dependent on those compliments in order to experience a glimpse of happiness. To become the Cause of our good feelings, we must believe that we are praiseworthy regardless of our clothing or our haircut. When we feel good from the inside out—before we receive any compliments—then we are acting as the Cause in our lives.

Being the Cause doesn't mean that we've become indifferent to the world. Emotions are an invaluable part of life. Our goal is to focus in on our ability to recognize our emotions when they do arise and train our minds to work in the gap between stimulus and response. It is in this space that we can connect to the Light and rise above reflex reactions that do more harm than good. This is the true meaning of transformation.

Let's look at a hypothetical example of how transformation of this nature might occur. Imagine in this first scenario that fifty thousand dollars in small bills is lying on top of a desk in an office. A man walks in and sees the money. After confirming that no one else is around, he scoops up the cash and flees like a bandit.

Now let's move to our second scenario, in which another man walks in and sees the fifty thousand dollars. He gets nervous being near all that money, begins to panic, and flees the building like a criminal.

In the third scenario a man walks in and sees the stack of bills. He gets excited and decides to steal the money. He looks around to make sure that no one is looking, scoops up the cash, and darts out the door. But then he stops. After agonizing for a moment, he decides to return the money to the desk.

Here's our fourth and final scenario: A man walks in and sees the money. Knowing that it will likely be stolen if it's left lying there, he places it inside a briefcase and hands the briefcase over to the authorities for safekeeping. Then he leaves a note on the desk asking whoever has misplaced a large sum of cash to contact him, and he will direct that person to the authorities.

Which man's behavior most closely resembles how you would respond under the same circumstances? Taking into account what we have learned thus far, which scenario reveals the most spiritual Light? In which situation is the man the Cause and not the Effect? The answer may surprise you. Let's examine each man's actions.

In the first scenario, the man is governed solely by his reactive, instinctive *Desire to Receive*, which tells him to take the money and run. Because of his reactive behavior, he is unable to receive the Light of fulfillment in his life. He is the Effect, not the Cause.

In the second scenario, the man is merely reacting to his instinctive "flight" instinct which tells him to run. Light is not revealed in this way, so the man enters the building and leaves it again with his nature unchanged.

In the third scenario, the man initially reacts to his desire to steal the cash, but then, in that all-important moment before a decision is made, he stops. By pausing, he shuts down his *Desire to Receive*, goes against his initial instinct, and transforms his nature—all within the space of a second. By returning the money, he makes himself the Cause of his own destiny—not the Effect of a suitcase full of money! His transformation from reactive to proactive reveals spiritual Light.

In the fourth scenario the man approaches the situation from a proactive state of mind to begin with. Because his instinct from the start is to do the honorable thing, his nature remains the same throughout the situation. Although his behavior is praiseworthy, his behavior brings him no additional Light, according to Kabbalah. He does have an opportunity to reveal Light, however. After returning the money, he must resist the temptation to act on his ego, which tells him he is morally better than most. He must resist his *Desire to Receive*—which in this case means his *desire to receive* praise for his good deed. His opportunity for transformation lies not in the physical act of returning the money, but rather in keeping his good deed to himself.

The moral of this story is that our positive traits are *not* what reveal Light. This is not to say that if you have transformed a reactive trait into a positive one in the past, that the Light you created then has since evaporated. Not at all! The Light you have revealed in your past continues to imbue your Vessel. It is not going anywhere. But the only way to accumulate more Light is by identifying, uprooting, and transforming your reactive negative characteristics into proactive positive characteristics. What ultimately determines our level of fulfillment is how much we resist our inherent nature. The more we resist, the more fulfillment we will feel.

To further illustrate this I'd like to share an updated version of a traditional Kabbalah tale, "The Wise Man and the Ten Thieves." It goes like this:

*In a small town in the Midwest there lived a mail carrier named Hank. He and his wife Jackie had only one child, a son named Brian. When Brian turned seven, a mysterious illness took hold of the boy. With each passing day he grew weaker. Hank drove hundreds of miles to visit countless doctors, but to no avail. Time was running out for young Brian, and Jackie could sense the angel of* death hovering over her baby boy's bedroom as he slept. It would take a miracle to save Brian's life.

It so happened that a wise old man lived in the same town. He was not a doctor, but he was known for his home remedies, which had worked wonders on any number of ailments and diseases. Many believed he could talk to angels and that their counsel was what enabled him to be so effective. Hank was at the end of his rope, so in a state of both skepticism and desperation, he knocked on the old man's door.

The wise man was greatly saddened to hear about Brian's dire situation. Hank begged him to work his magic on his dying son, and in response, the healer took Hank's hand in his and promised to do the best he could.

That night the old man ascended high into the spirit world, using prayers and meditations known only to a few. When he reached the gates of Heaven, he was shocked to find that the gates were locked. The fate of the little boy had already been set.

The night soon passed, and the morning sun began to rise in the eastern sky over this quaint Midwestern town. The old sage met Hank outside the post office. With tears in his eyes, the old man delivered the news.

"I'm afraid that the fate of your son has already been decided," the sage said. "There is nothing I can do."

The crushing blow brought Hank to his knees. He begged the old man, "Please, I have nowhere else to turn! Brian is my only child, and you are my only hope!"

*The old mystic did not have the heart to resist the cries of this tormented man. He replied, "I will make one more attempt, but please understand, I cannot promise anything." Hank thanked him profusely, and they parted ways.*

*An unusual idea occurred to the old man. It was a long shot, but he realized that he had nothing to lose and the precious life of a young boy to gain. So quickly he summoned his young assistant and requested that he travel to the nearest city and bring back ten hardened criminals. The assistant was shocked by the request, but he knew better than to question a man who could talk to angels.*

*"Find me the worst scoundrels possible, the lowest of the low," the old man repeated. "And please, hurry!"*

*The assistant drove into the city, and to his surprise, he was able to gather together ten thieves quite quickly. In fact, he was amazed at how readily they agreed to accompany him to the home of the old healer. Apparently, this master's powers were quite well known even outside his small town.*

*The assistant and his sordid band of ex-cons arrived at the house of the old man, who thanked them for coming and invited them all into his home. Some of the worst criminals in the country sat around his living room, boastfully swapping their favorite crime stories. Then the old man motioned for them to be silent. They all listened respectfully as he asked these men to share his prayers, and made his specific request.*

*The next morning, as the town's roosters jubilantly shattered the morning silence, Hank the mail carrier could be*

seen dancing wildly down Main Street. A car pulled up alongside the ecstatic man. Behind the wheel was the old man's assistant, and in the back seat sat the old sage. "My dear friend," he exclaimed, "it appears that you have good news to share."

"I thank you with all my heart!" cried the mail carrier. "My beautiful boy Brian received a miracle overnight. It's as though he was never sick at all. He awoke before dawn feeling better than ever!"

"Indeed, this is wonderful news," said the old man. "Be well, my friend!" And the car drove off.

Perplexed, the assistant turned to his mentor in the back seat. "How were you able to perform a miracle in the company of such thieves?" And this is how the sage replied:

"When I prayed that first night for our friend and his only son, I saw that the gates of Heaven were locked. There was nothing I could do. But how could I refuse to help when he pleaded with me so desperately to try again? That's when the idea of sending you out to find the criminals came to me."

The assistant was confused. "What could the criminals do for you that you couldn't already do yourself?" he asked.

The mystic broke into a wide smile and replied. "You see, a good thief knows all about breaking and entering. I brought them with me to the gates of Heaven and they were able to pick all the locks! When these criminals broke in, my prayers were able to make their way into the Divine Sanctuary, where they were finally answered!"

This story is one of my all-time favorites. Can you see how the old man represents all of our most positive traits, while the thieves represent all of our negative, egocentric traits? After all, we are all thieves to one degree or another. As we see in the story, we all have virtuous qualities, but these alone are not enough to create miracles. It's when our negative attributes are transformed into Light that we gain the keys to Heaven. This is because when we identify and work to transform our self-centered qualities, blessings and good fortune become free to flow into our lives.

Another lesson to be found here lies in the willingness of the sage to keep trying in the face of desperate odds. When practicing transformation, we can't be afraid to fail. Mistakes are inevitable; we are human beings, after all! The good news is that we actually reveal more Light when we fall and get back up again. That's because when we climb back up we are overcoming our ego's tendency to wallow in misery.

If we never fall, we have no opportunities for transformation, and as a result we stay exactly where we are. What fun is there in never moving forward, in being stagnant, in playing it safe all of the time? Sounds pretty dull, if you ask me. Sure, failing can be hard on our self-esteem—*if* we allow it to be. How about instead of beating yourself up for making a mistake, you respond by being kind to yourself? In fact, why not make falling a cause for celebration?

Even Michael Jordan made a mistake or two in his illustrious career, but that just made him all the more remarkable by reminding us that he was human, like you or me. He just knew how to tap into a power that exists for all of us. Sure, he could have been a good basketball player without plugging into the 99 Percent Realm. His game would have been impressive, but without challenging himself to resist the easy shot and to dig deeper, would he have 'blown us away' like he did? I don't think so. In much the same way, it's only when we decide to take our game to the next level that we start to see mind-blowing changes in our own lives.

- Before every decision there exists a moment in which we can choose to respond proactively or reactively.

- Our ego thrives on reactive behavior, because reactive behavior keeps us disconnected from the Light.

- Contrary to the ego's message, the world does not revolve around us.

- When we transform our behavior from reactive to proactive, we receive the type of fulfillment that can only come from the Light.

- Don't be afraid to fall. Picking ourselves up after a fall produces more Light than if we'd never fallen at all.

Take a piece of paper and divide it into four columns lengthwise. In the first column, write down three recent instances in which you reacted to a person or a situation. In the second column, jot down the emotions that were triggered by each experience. And in the third column, make note of the physical actions that took place in each situation. Be as specific as you can. If your reaction seems embarrassing to you now, even better! That just means you have more room to grow. Now consider ways in which you could act more proactively in the future. Write down some of those ideas in column four.

# there's no use blaming other people or external events

**Y**ou've been invited to attend a dance, and lacking appropriate attire you ask your friend if you can borrow some great-looking clothes for the occasion. Your friend is hesitant to loan you a favorite outfit, but finally goes along when you promise that you will treat the outfit as if it were made of Egyptian silk.

Off you go to the dance. You are having a magnificent time, and you're feeling so good that when an acquaintance invites you and your date back to their house for an after-hours party, you readily agree.

The party is a blast until things start to get a little rowdy. You decide to stick it out when someone bumps your elbow, and the next thing you know, you have spilled a full glass of red wine all over your friend's beloved clothes. *How could this have happened? You think. Everything was going so well! If that other person hadn't been drunk and unable to walk straight, I wouldn't be in this mess.*

The next day you drop the clothing off at your friend's house. You try to explain the circumstances of the evening and how someone who obviously wasn't thinking clearly plowed right into you at the party. Your friend, unconvinced, informs you that the outfit is most likely ruined and the only one to blame is you!

But how can this be? You were merely an innocent bystander, after all. Or were you? Each moment of that evening contained a choice—not necessarily a choice that you liked (and certainly not a choice your ego liked), but a choice nonetheless. You chose to go to the dance and have a great time, and you chose to go to the party afterwards.

Going to the party wasn't necessarily a "bad" decision. In fact, according to Kabbalah there is no right and wrong; only a variety of different outcomes. There's every possibility that if that person hadn't accidentally bumped into you, the outfit would have been returned in the same perfect condition in which your friend loaned it to you. But that's not how the evening unfolded. Your choices led you to the moment in which events went awry. It may be a bitter pill to swallow at the time, but *you and you alone* are responsible for the evening's outcome.

Admittedly, taking responsibility for your actions is bound to feel uncomfortable at first, but in the long run you will be amazed by the life-altering results. When you become accountable for yourself, you have the power to make changes if you don't like the outcome. By tweaking your behavior based on taking full responsibility for the way events unfold, you literally transform yourself and your life.

On the other hand, when you shirk responsibility for your mistakes, what chance do you have of improving your life? If you talk yourself into believing that mitigating circumstances or someone else is always to blame, how will you ever learn to take responsibility? In other words, if you keep thinking that something outside yourself—some external factor—must change in order for you to be happy, then you are going to be waiting an awfully long time! I can't remember a situation when my external environment changed simply because I wanted it to. Transformation requires action. And action starts with taking responsibility.

This is how many of us approach our lives—by waiting around for our luck to change. But as you have learned by now, life does not happen to you; you happen to life!

So how does your life look and feel to you right at this moment? I ask this pointed question not to get you thinking critically about yourself, but to encourage you to take an open-minded look at where you are in your life. The more you own up to your mistakes and weaknesses, the more fuel you will have for your transformational journey. Remember, utilizing our existing positive traits won't bring us the fulfillment we seek—only turning our negatives into positives will do the trick. So rather than pretend your negative traits don't exist, own up to them. That's the all-important first step. And then transform them.

One tell-tale sign that you are not ready or willing to own up to your circumstances is if you find yourself engaged in "If only" thinking. *If only my parents understood how hard my classes were.... If only my ADD didn't flare up during Algebra class.... If only I didn't have to ride the bus to school, the kids wouldn't tease me...."* If only" thinking is one way we shift blame onto someone or something else. When we catch ourselves doing this we can ask ourselves, "What can I do to change the outcome here? What is my role in the situation and how can I change it?" By asking ourselves these questions—*and by answering them honestly*—we start becoming the Cause and stop being the Effect. Consider these suggestions as tricks of the trade. Everyone—and I mean everyone—needs some pointers in this Game called Life.

That's what Kabbalah calls life, the Ultimate Game. No one is new to playing games. No matter where you are from—no matter what your socioeconomic background, your religion, or ethnicity—your childhood included various kinds of games. When you won—which was always the objective—you gained a palpable sense of satisfaction, and when you lost, you were disappointed. Winning was everything.

But was it really, or did it merely *seem* like it was? Let's go back to the Vessel for a moment. In one sense, the Vessel just kept winning and winning and winning. But because of the Bread of Shame that kept accumulating, the Vessel never felt satisfied. So it wasn't really winning then, was it? In order to truly win and to have a chance to take home the grand prize of everlasting joy, the Vessel had to decide to resist the Light. The same holds true for us. Imagine playing a game in which the whole competition was rigged so that you couldn't lose. No matter how poorly you played, you'd still magically earn enough points to win. How much enjoyment do you think you would derive from such a game? My guess is not much. I say that because I know that I'd be bored out of my mind—maybe even frustrated and angry, to boot. If I didn't stand a chance at losing, then winning would have no meaning. What's the point of playing if you are guaranteed to win every time?

In order to experience a fair fight, you need to have an opponent who stands a chance of beating you. In Kabbalah, the opponent is called the Satan, pronounced, suh-*tahn*, with the accent on the second syllable. I emphasize this point because I don't want you thinking that we are talking about the little red monster with horns and a pitchfork. That little man is folklore, while the Satan I'm talking about is as real as it gets, even though you can't see or touch him.

Satan is another one of the kabbalistic code words I mentioned earlier. The name Satan stands for the ego, or the reactive tendencies that we all have. The *Zohar*, the major text of Kabbalah written about two thousand years ago, identified Satan as a force that challenges us to become our best. The *Zohar* revealed some of Satan's oft-used weapons and strategies. Satan is the voice in our heads that encourages us to do something we know we absolutely shouldn't do. Satan is the voice that talks us out of taking an action that we know we must take. And, worst of all, Satan is the voice that feeds us every reason why we shouldn't apply Resistance and rid ourselves of our reactive behavior once and for all.

Why does the Opponent, Satan, work so hard? Because by ridding ourselves of our reactive behavior, we would be ridding ourselves of him! And he would much prefer to continue taking up residence in the comfy confines of your mind. He will do everything in his power to convince you, his host, that he and you are one and the same and that what he has to say is relevant and true. But, the reality is that he has only lies to tell.

Satan, the ego, the Opponent—these are all names for the chaos that exists in the physical world and in the human psyche. Satan is the one who prompts us to point our accusatory fingers at one another. He is the one responsible for our feelings of anxiety, fear, uncertainty, doubt, and confusion. So, why on Earth do we want to continue hosting a houseguest like this? We don't, and that's precisely why it's time that we give him the boot.

But let's be practical here. Before we can effectively battle Satan, we need to understand his game plan. Only by knowing his shiftiest maneuvers can we learn to outsmart him. That being said, let's consider some examples of ways in which the Opponent persuades us to follow his will.

- Your best friend tells you something extremely personal and swears you to secrecy. But a few days later, after being unexpectedly included in a gossip session with the some popular kids from your class, you find yourself divulging your friend's secret. Although you enjoyed the attention that came from sharing such a juicy tidbit of information, afterwards you feel terrible about what you have done.

- All semester you've been doing your geometry homework with a friend, but the truth is that you haven't really learned a thing, because you've just been copying her answers. The final is coming in two weeks, which gives you enough time to get a handle on the material. But it would be so much easier if you just waited until the night before the test when you and your friend usually meet and you could get her "help" then.

- You promised your father you would have dinner with him and his new wife, but a girl who you have been interested in dating has invited some friends over to her house while her parents are away. You can't pass up an opportunity like this to get to know her, so you cancel dinner at the last minute.

• You accidentally see one of your classmates throwing up in the bathroom, and you sense that she practices this behavior often. You know you should tell the school counselor, but you don't want to get your friend in trouble.

• Your best friend smokes marijuana but has decided to quit. He asks you to come over and hang out so he can keep his mind off of smoking. You want to help him out, especially since he's been there for you when you needed it, but there's a big party that night with some important people attending. Besides, he's practically an adult, you think. He can make it through one night without picking up the habit again.

• A friend who you've grown up with moves out of your neighborhood into a large home in a new subdivision. Big houses never mattered to you before, but now that your friend is living large in what is practically a mansion, you can't help but feel resentful. Your house suddenly seems like a shanty and your new friend like a snob.

Do you see Satan in any of these examples? If we honestly examine our responses to situations like these, we can inevitably find the breadcrumbs that lead straight to the Opponent. Once we do, we can hunt him down and strip him of his power. Doing so will probably cause us some discomfort, but it's only temporary. We risk a lot more discomfort if we continue to play into the Opponent's wishes.

When Satan came into being, one of his first moves was to manipulate the DNA of the *Desire to Receive*. Before him, the *Desire to Receive* just wanted Light and could seamlessly be transformed into the *Desire to Share*. But the Opponent changed this. He turned the *Desire to Receive* into the *Desire to Receive for the Self Alone*. Like a growing sinkhole, this desire can consume everything in its vicinity so that even spiritual Light cannot escape its grasp!

We've all experienced this desire—and most likely have felt lousy in the process. If your friend shows up wearing a pair of high-end athletic shoes and your heart skips a beat because you have had your eye on those shoes for awhile, this is the *Desire to Receive*. Now this desire is not immediately dangerous in and of itself, but it can become harmful when we act on it. If, for example, you become resentful of your friend for purchasing the new shoes before you, then you are acting on the *Desire to Receive for the Self Alone*, and you are at risk of losing your friend—not to mention an opportunity to reveal Light by taking the high road and resisting your jealous inclinations.

Resisting the Opponent and the *Desire to Receive for the Self Alone* all starts in our mind. The mind is the Opponent's playing field, so we have to fight him on his own turf. Those are the rules. Take a moment now and point to your mind. Most likely you pointed to your head, to your brain. But are the brain and the mind the same thing? The brain is a physical organ that can be removed and dissected. Is the same true of the mind?

Imagine a primitive tribesman venturing out of the jungle with no knowledge whatsoever of the modern world. He comes across a transistor radio playing music and looks at it in astonishment, believing that the box is the source of the music. He opens up the radio and accidentally pulls out the battery. The music stops. He thinks he has killed some miraculous creature, but of course we know that the source of the music is really a radio station broadcasting many miles away.

Our thoughts do not originate within the wetware of the brain, just as the music did not originate from within the wires and speakers of the radio. Instead, the brain is like an antenna, a receiving station that picks up a signal and then relays it to the conscious mind. And there are two cosmic broadcasters: the Light and Satan. When we learn to tell them apart, our lives become exponentially more enjoyable!

Here are a few tips to help you discern which broadcasts you are receiving. You'll know that the broadcast is coming from Satan if:

1. Your thoughts seem logical and rational;
2. The broadcast is loud and clear;
3. The thought urges you to react to a situation.

By contrast, you can tell that the broadcast is emanating from the Light if:

1. The broadcast is faint and barely audible;
2. You receive a sudden flash of intuition or inspiration;
3. Meaningful information appears in your dreams.

It's important to know that, like the Light, the radio station of Satan broadcasts twenty-four hours a day, seven days a week. But just because this station is on all of the time, does not mean we have to listen to it. As with everything else in life, we have a choice. But know that the Opponent will work non-stop to push his station on you. He'll play all of the right commercials featuring the most enticing products. His music will sound great, but if we listen carefully we'll notice that his lyrics do not make us feel happy. Yet we can experience ultimate joy, despite Satan's non-stop chatter; we do this by blocking his airwaves from entering our consciousness.

One kabbalistic tool you can use for this is called the Transformation Formula. We've discussed it in general terms, but now I'd like to show you how to use it more specifically:

1. A challenge occurs.
2. Realize that the Opponent—not the challenge—is the real enemy and that the Opponent is, in fact, your ego encouraging you to react.
3. In order to allow the Light in, shut down your reactive system.
4. Express your proactive nature. See yourself as the Cause, as the creator, as a being of sharing.

The moment of transformation takes place during steps three and four. This is when you are able to plug into the 99 Percent Realm and experience the Light.

I bet you are thinking, *Sure, this formula sounds helpful, but how does it work in real life?* Let's say you're at track practice when one of your teammates approaches you and starts giving you the third degree about something that you know nothing about. Fellow students nearby overhear bits and pieces of her tirade. You're clueless, but you feel your blood start to boil anyway. Before you know it, you find yourself yelling right back at her. And it feels good, too! That's how reactive behavior works—it feels exhilarating for a moment as the endorphins flood our brain. But then the feeling dissipates leaving us feeling worn-out and just as frustrated as we were before we reacted in the first place, if not more so.

Let's apply the Transformation Formula to this situation and see how things might play out if we tune in to the Light and ignore the messages of Satan.

1. A challenge occurs. Your friend blows up at you at practice.
2. Realize that your *reaction* is the real enemy. Your feelings of anger, hurt, and frustration are what you truly need to confront, not your friend.
3. Shut down your reactive system to allow the Light in. Tap into that split-second pause before a decision is made. Let go of all your emotional reactions. Instead of shouting back,

become an observer. Let your friend vent, even if you're not to blame. What matters isn't who is right or wrong. What matters is your decision not to react.

4. Become the Cause. Take responsibility for being part of this moment. Your friend is bringing up an issue that applies to you in some way. Perhaps the situation is helping you to see how much emphasis you place on what people around you are thinking, or how quick you are to anger. Honor the gift you are receiving, and then observe that the rest of this moment is about your friend. What's the best thing you can do for her in this moment? Perhaps you can find a quiet place to ask her calmly, "What's wrong?"

If you follow these steps, I can guarantee that you will experience the 99 Percent Realm. And as you move forward, your actions increasingly reflecting the Light of the Creator, you will see some surprising changes in your circumstances. Your friend, for instance, might respond in a way that you never dreamed possible. Perhaps she'll tell you that she is under a lot of pressure at home, or that she has been struggling with depression.

All day long, people and situations trigger reactions within us. Another student has parked in your assigned parking spot in the high school student lot. Or you find out that you didn't make the cheerleading squad but your best friend did. Maybe you discover that your older brother has "borrowed" money from you again, without asking. Or your dad and mom got into a noisy, late-night argument last night. You may believe that you are powerless over these external circumstances. And you are. *But you are not powerless over Satan, and he is the real enemy.* You have the tools at your command to counter his every move, and, most importantly, you have the Light to protect you.

I didn't drink or do drugs when I was in junior high and high school, but there were certainly those around me who did. As I mentioned earlier, I wasn't exactly inundated with invitations to party. Even when those opportunities did present themselves, those situations were never easy. Believe me, during much of my teen years I wanted more than anything to be one of the "cool" kids, to be included and accepted. Doing drugs would have been an easy way in for me—not to mention that drugs might have helped ease the loneliness I felt around my classmates and given me more confidence around girls.

Pot was the drug of choice when I was in junior high, but in high school it became cocaine. Kids who tried it said that the effects were euphoric and that you felt as if you were at one with God. That sounded an awful lot like the 99 Percent Realm, so my curiosity was piqued. But by this time I had internalized enough kabbalistic wisdom to know that Satan always speaks with impeccable logic! My parents had raised me to honor my intuition, which told me that lasting fulfillment could not be found in a pill, white powder, or a joint.

Despite the temptation of drugs, I chose not to take that path. Instead, I used the Transformation Formula to resist the temptation. What was my challenge? The kid in front of me offering me a moment of pleasure in the form of a drug! My reaction? Desire was my reaction. Who doesn't want to experience pleasure? I could easily have just said "Yes," but instead I tuned into that split second in time in which a decision is made. Then I resisted my desire. I didn't make up excuses; I simply said, No, thanks.

I would like to say that my popularity soared because of my proactive behavior. Not a chance! I was right back on the outside looking in. But in that moment of Resistance—in that flash when I recognized that my craving was simply the Opponent—I was fully connected with the 99 Percent Realm. And once you experience *that* 'high,' nothing less will ever do. It makes you all the more determined to figure out how you make that incredible feeling last. And you can.

Here's how: Stop pacifying Satan. Resist his advances. Attack any and every message he sends your way. And practice the Transformation Formula as much as possible. When you do this repeatedly, you will experience the Light more and more until the Light becomes a familiar part of your life. The amount of Light you experience is directly proportionate to the effort you put towards battling the Opponent. It's that simple. The actual work might be hard, but in principle, your strategy for ultimate success couldn't be more straightforward.

You can read this book a thousand times, but if you don't practice what you are reading the words will merely remain ink on paper. And Satan will only grow stronger. Any good soldier knows that you don't go into battle without training first. Skip training, and you doom your mission to failure. So think of this book as training for your quiet, inner self as you prepare it for the fight of your life, the one against the Opponent.

- Our thoughts, words, and actions are entirely our responsibility.

- As soon as we place blame on someone or something else, we make it the Cause and ourselves the Effect. Pointing fingers takes away all of our power to change the situation we're in.

- We must have an Opponent in order to rid ourselves of Bread of Shame. Our Opponent is Satan, which is our ego and our reactive behavior.

- The voice of Satan is logical, rational, and loud. It urges us to react.

- The voice of the Light is intuitive, inspirational, and non-intrusive, and it often appears in our dreams. It encourages us to respond proactively.

- Use the Transformation Formula:
  1. An obstacle occurs.
  2. Realize that your reaction (the Opponent) is the enemy and that the Opponent is, in fact, your ego.
  3. Shut down your reactive system to allow the Light in.
  4. Express your proactive nature.

- We are able to connect to the 99 Percent Realm between steps three and four. This is the moment of transformation.

Learning to distinguish the voice of the Light from the voice of the Satan is essential to living a life of joy and ful-fillment. So let's start with the Light. Write down the last dream you had in as much detail as you can remember. There's no need to engage your critical self here—no edit-ing or interpreting allowed! Simply write down what hap-pened. Even though the message behind the images might not be clear right now, it's important to recognize that they are part of the 99 Percent Realm. The more credence you give your dreams, the more attuned you will become to "hearing" the Light's broadcast. Your dreams will start to make a lot more sense, and, over time, your life will too!

Now write down the last time you had a gut feeling about something. Even if it was just a faint knowing that some-thing positive or negative might happen, that still counts. Go into as much detail as possible. How did having that intuition make your body feel? How did your mind register it? Did you act on the hunch? And if so, what happened? If not, what happened, and what might have happened if you had? As always, this is not an exercise in self-judgment. The goal is that by writing down your intuitive experiences, you will open yourself to having more of them. And as you begin to understand these subtle messages more clearly, you will allow them to draw you closer to the Light.

Now let's check out your receptiveness to Satan's voice. Write down the last time you were swayed by an external event. No need to over-think this. Just go with your gut (I know you know how now!). Write down what form your obstacle took. Be sure to make note of your emotional reaction as well as your outward behavior. How did you feel when this interaction was complete?

Now rewrite the scenario, this time applying the Transformation Formula. Your obstacle will remain the same, as will your emotional reaction. But imagine a scenario in which you shut down your reactive system to allow in the Light and acted proactively instead. Now write that scenario down. Go through these steps with at least one more example. By allowing yourself to respond differently on paper, you are effectively training yourself to respond differently in real life. Remember, you can't go into battle if you don't practice your maneuvers first. You're one defeated man or woman if you try to do so!

**resistance is the
only direct route
to the light**

**S**atan has a powerful weapon up his sleeve, one with which we are all intimately familiar. That weapon is time. But time is an illusion. It doesn't exist in the 99 Percent Realm, and it didn't exist before the physical world came into being. In the 1 Percent Physical Realm in which we live, time creates the distance between Cause and Effect, between action and reaction.

Without the illusion of time, past, present, and future would all collapse into one, which is how things are in the 99 Percent Realm. There is no "before and after," no "then and now." There is only oneness. Imagine you are on a train twenty cars long and sitting in the tenth car, which represents the present moment. Cars one through nine represent the past. Cars eleven through twenty represent your future. What do you perceive right now, with your five senses? Only your immediate surroundings in the tenth car. You cannot see the cars ahead of you, or the cars behind. So your logical mind (and we know now who is behind logical thinking) convinces you that the tenth car is all that exists. But the truth is that all of the cars—past, present, and future— exist simultaneously as part of one train. If you could float outside the train, viewing things from the 99 Percent Realm, you would see every one of the cars, from beginning to caboose, all at once!

We owe much of our suffering to time. Thoughts of the past often fill us with sadness or regret, while thoughts of the future can bring anxiety and fear; this leaves the present moment the only safe place for our minds to go, yet most people don't allow their focus to remain on the here and now. It, too, can seem overwhelming and scary. So where does *that* leave us?

Consider this: In the time it took you to read the previous sentence, your future became your present and your present became your past. In other words, past, present, and future all merged into one. Such is the case with every moment. If we embrace the notion that time is merely an illusion of the 1 Percent physical world, we would find many of our demands and expectations melting away—and with them, much of our suffering.

When I was in high school, one of my parents' friends was diagnosed with terminal cancer. For the first few weeks after having received the news, she vacillated between anger and sadness. But not long afterward, I remember having a conversation with her and was surprised to find her in good spirits. What was her secret? Her diagnosis had prompted her to see each moment she had on this Earth as precious. She no longer took a single breath for granted, and her tendency to dwell on thoughts of the past or the future had evaporated along with any fear or anger she felt in the beginning. She was like a new woman! Stories like these are not uncommon. When people are faced with the prospect of dying, often they become keenly aware of the gift of life that they have been given in the present moment.

Our physical bodies won't last forever. It's easy to forget this, especially when we are young and feel invincible. I hadn't given much thought to the notion of mortality until my parent's friend became ill. But her experience left quite an impression on me. I was struck by how peaceful she became when she realized that her days were numbered. All of our days are limited, and rarely do we know just how much time we have left. My parents' friend actually went on to live for several more years, and while she had her ups and downs, her rich appreciation of the present moment stayed with her.

How good are you at staying in the present moment? If you are like most people, you probably could use some practice. Experiment with training your mind to give its full attention to the here and now. Simply experience this moment. No excuses. No distractions. Now consider how your body feels. How comfortable are you? Can you hear traffic or a neighbor's radio playing? What thought is at the forefront of your mind? Observe that thought without judgment. This is what it feels like to *just be* with yourself—nothing more, nothing less.

Satan does not want us to be with ourselves. There is far too much truth in the present moment for his liking. And with truth comes the potential for transformation, which is absolutely the last thing Satan wants for us. He would prefer that our minds be preoccupied with regrets about the past and worries about the future. A distracted mind makes for a weakened opponent. But we can take back our power right here. Starting now. It's okay if your mind starts to wander. But be aware of where it takes you; more importantly, be aware that this is the Opponent distracting you from your true path. Consider that time is merely a weapon in his extensive arsenal.

The Opponent also uses another hidden aspect of time to his advantage. Because time offers us some legroom between action and reaction, it supports the idea that bad deeds go unpunished and good deeds go unrewarded. Your friend drives home drunk and makes it home without a scratch, while your aunt gets in a wreck while delivering meals to the elderly. It just doesn't add up.

The delay created by time makes it difficult for us to see the interconnectedness of all things. It might have been years ago that we planted a negative seed with an act of cruelty or a harsh word, so by the time the seed sprouts, we've forgotten all about it. But just because we've forgotten doesn't mean that the effects of our actions won't materialize at some point along the way. It might seem to happen "all of a sudden," but you and I both know now that everything has a reason. There is always a Cause. Chaos only appears to be sudden because time has separated Cause and Effect.

Your aunt's wreck, which seemed to come out of nowhere, happened because of actions that she took weeks, months, or years ago. In the same way, your friend who seems to get off scot-free with his impaired driving, will at some point face a consequence. Maybe not today. Maybe not tomorrow. But his drunk driving is planting a seed for the future—and it is not a healthy one. At some point, we must all face the consequences of our actions—large or small, good or bad. It might take days, weeks, months, decades, or even lifetimes, but repercussions are inevitable.

One thing to keep in mind is that in any given moment it is impossible to know if you are seeing a good or a bad seed coming to fruition. For instance, your aunt may have been locked in a cycle of doing too much for others and not enough for herself. Maybe her life has been chaotic for years—that is, until she had her car wreck. What seems like a totally unfair turn of events (after all, she was doing volunteer work when the wreck occurred!) might be exactly what she needs to turn her life around. In a matter of seconds she has been taught that she must learn to slow down and take care of herself first before she can take care of others. Knowing this, would you say that the car wreck was a positive or negative event? Along the exact same lines, was the cancer from which my parent's friend suffered beneficial or detrimental? Think about it.

The Opponent also challenges our faith by delaying access to the Light. If we have resisted a reaction but we do not experience the Light immediately, we may feel ripped off or perhaps begin to doubt the value of Kabbalah and our spiritual work. *Why bother?* We might think. *If we never reap the benefit of our good deeds, what's the point?* Because time separates Cause from Effect, it creates a convincing illusion that they're not connected.

If you cheat on a test in biology class, the chaos may show up in your personal life rather than in your studies—but it's still showing up. If you lie to your father, the effect may be seen in your physical health, or your social life. You may bully your class-mates all through junior high with no apparent consequences for your actions. But that doesn't mean you have safely eluded them. The effects may manifest 30 years from now when you lose your life savings due to a gambling addiction, or when your child contracts a life-threatening illness. Similarly, volunteering to take in stray animals doesn't guarantee that a dog will never bite you. But your good work might plant the seed for that wonderful job opportunity in the field of social work. You just never know. But there is one thing for certain: Your every action creates an effect that will eventually come back to you. Cosmically, we get away with nothing.

When the Light we generate through proactive behavior at school materializes at home, Satan will try to distract us so much that we don't even notice how well we are suddenly getting along with our parents. When the Light does not materialize as a date to homecoming or as a lead in the school musical, we may assume that our proactive behavior is getting us nowhere. The Opponent limits our perspective, and when we miss the big picture we fail to recognize the Light that is shining abundantly in our lives.

Satan's greatest strength lies in his power to confuse us. He makes us forget that he is the Opponent, all the while convincing us that our friends, our loved ones, our classmates, and our teachers are the ones who are out to get us. He feeds us a convincing story about how everyone else is to blame, but that's all it is—a story.

Try this: the next time you feel as if you're being wronged, imagine the Opponent standing right in front of you, whispering into your tormentor's ear! See that person falling under the sway of the masterful Opponent. And imagine the Opponent laughing and growing stronger at the chaos he is unleashing. There's no doubt about it—he is having the time of his life! But you can pull the rug out from underneath him in a heartbeat. How? Resist your desire to react!

Resistance is necessary to produce both Light with a capital "L," as well as light with a lowercase "l." When kabbalists speak of Light with a capital "L," they are referring to the infinite Light of the Creator. When they speak of light with a lowercase "l," they are referring to conventional light such as light from the sun or from a light bulb. Both Light and light share the property of providing illumination.

A light bulb generates light using three components: a positive pole (+), a negative pole (–), and a filament separating the (+) from the (–). The filament actually plays the most crucial role within the bulb, because it acts as a resistor, pushing back the current flowing from the positive to keep it from connecting directly with the negative. This resistance is what makes the light bulb work. Now think of the Vessel as the negative pole, the Light as the positive, and the filament as the Vessel's act of Resistance. By consistently pushing back the incoming energy, the Vessel has become the creator of its own Light!

We are the resistors in our own lives. By consistently refusing to entertain the Opponent's scripts, stories, and lies, we create lasting Light. And not just flickers here and there. No, I'm talking about steady Light that can stand the test of time, and never fades.

- Past, present, and future co-exist. There is no separation among them.

- In order to divert our attention from the present moment, Satan uses our belief that time is divided. He tricks us by delaying consequences, which fosters doubt about the consequences of our actions.

- Satan has a talent for confusing us. He convinces us that the Opponent is everyone else *but* him, and he makes us forget that our own reactive behavior is the real Opponent.

- There is an Effect for every Cause. Every action, good or bad, plants a seed, and every seed will bear fruit—even if it takes weeks, months, years, or lifetimes.

- It is the filament's ongoing resistance between positive and negative poles that creates the light within a light bulb. By consistently resisting our reactive behavior, we create continuous Light in the same way.

**exercise:** I'd be surprised if you haven't been presented with some recent opportunities to resist your own reactive behavior. Take the time now to list some recent examples, and be as specific as you can. In some cases, your efforts will have brought you the outcome you hoped for, while in others your behavior will still be reactive despite your best efforts. That's okay—no one is born a saint! After listing your recent moments of Resistance, make a note of how you felt during and after each situation. How did your body feel? Your mind? Your spirit? Take a moment now and compare these notes with those from Chapter Five. Look for places of overlap, as well as places of growth. Can you see tangible ways in which resisting has already improved your quality of life? Make note of these. Each one of these moments is like a photon of Light. Now, imagine collecting enough of these photons so that you are encircled by an uninterrupted glow of light at all times. That is our goal and the goal of Kabbalah.

**despite the initial sparks, reactive behavior always ends in burnout**

**R**eactive behavior is the most efficient pathway to pleasure. It's instant gratification. An immediate buzz. A runner's high. A much-anticipated release. A shot of endorphins into the bloodstream. Reactive behavior can feel incredible—for the moment.

Here's what happens: When we opt for instant gratification, we create a very bright light. A direct connection occurs between our reactive desire (the negative pole) and the Light (the positive pole), producing a momentary flash of pleasure followed by darkness: the sequence of events is not unlike a light bulb whose filament has burned out. Electricity works according to the unseen laws of the universe, not unlike gravity. If you jump out of an airplane with or without a parachute, there's nowhere to go but down due to the existence of gravity. The same holds true for electricity. Touch a live wire and you will get electrocuted—that's how the physical laws of this world work. You can't get around them.

When you connect directly with the Light without using Restriction, you recreate what happened in the very beginning—remember when the Vessel did nothing but receive Light? The result was Bread of Shame; there was no lasting fulfillment to be had. In the same way, every time you immediately satisfy your desire you flood yourself with Light, create Bread of Shame, and burn out. But that immediate delight can be so seductive that we find ourselves chasing after it again and again.

One of the reasons I didn't do drugs, smoke cigarettes, or mess around with alcohol in high school was because I was fortunate enough to recognize (thanks to Kabbalah) the consequences of an artificial high. Many people who have come to the Centre over the years were once drug addicts, or are still struggling to clean up. These people have often spent much of their lives trying to recreate a transitory moment of pleasure. But it's also true that those experiences are precisely what brought them to The Centre and to a turning point in their lives.

I remember spending one afternoon chatting with a man in his mid-thirties who had been hooked on Ecstasy since his teens. Although he was clean when we spoke, it wasn't easy for him. Every morning he had to renew his commitment to not take Ecstasy that day, and to resist the temporary pleasure it gave him. He explained to me that the first time he had taken the drug he had experienced a high unlike any other he had ever known, and ever since he had been trying to recreate that first amazing experience. But all of his efforts to do so had been in vain.

Drug addicts put themselves through terrible pain and suffering. They lose respect for themselves, so they can't respect the needs of others. Every time they snort, shoot up, or take those pills they take the path of least Resistance. For a brief moment, they touch the Light directly, and then they feel more desperate than they did before. Most addicts are aware of this, yet they still can't stop. They have become entangled in a powerful cycle of self-destruction that reduces them to being merely the effect of the drug. The drug has become the Cause and the creator of their lives.

Much like junkies, we become addicted to our reactive behaviors. We put ourselves through unnecessary pain and suffering by constantly chasing after that transient high. Perhaps we're searching for compliments or approval from others. Or maybe we get our high from spreading gossip, or dishing out sarcastic one-liners at the expense of others. Just as the man I mentioned before had to recommit each morning to staying clean, we must commit ourselves to practicing Resistance each day, because it is the only way to achieve consistent contact with the Light. In the beginning, we will make mistakes—that is a fact. But failure can become a path to success, *if* we keep trying. If you need incentive, remember that every time you assert your conscious intent to resist, you reveal more of the Light.

Artificial highs can come in many forms. For example, it's easy to become addicted to people and relationships. Have you ever felt like you couldn't live without a particular friend, family member, boyfriend, or girlfriend? Perhaps you and the person you were dating couldn't stop texting or calling one another; you just had to be in contact at all times, and when you weren't you felt sad. Certain songs, or a particular smell or type of clothing, would make you think of him or her when you were apart. And just the thought of losing this person made you feel sick to your stomach. And haven't you had times when it seemed impossible to get through a situation without a sister or a best friend? You needed this person in order to feel viable.

Whether we want to admit it or not, these types of thoughts and behaviors are addictive—even though they might seem grounded in love and devotion. The reason for their unhealthy nature is this: Our self-worth has become entangled in what *they* think of us, how *they* see us, and how we feel when we are with *them*. We've made another person the Cause, and we've allowed ourselves to become the Effect. And so we find ourselves running from the darkness we feel in between the highs, and toward the small bursts of pleasure that come from direct contact with the Light. As you may know, or can readily imagine, this is an exhausting way to live!

Addiction is not to be confused with affection. Having affection for someone—wishing that person happiness or freedom from suffering—is a Light-inspired desire, and that is precisely what we are striving for. With affection, we do not feel as if our very existence is dependent on another's. Addiction, on the other hand, feels like living in a vat of superglue. Without that special person, we feel utterly useless and unable to function. We may also feel as if we need to fix them, or vice versa. And although we might be addicted to the holding hands and the instant messaging, the fights, misunderstandings, and the drama have an equally addictive quality all on their own. It probably comes as no surprise that drama is a reactive behavior, too. Many people mistake it as proof of love, but it is merely another form of instant gratification.

When we are continually reacting to people and events, our mind is churning so fast that we don't allow ourselves the opportunity to explore it, to befriend it, and to tame it. A racing mind that is ruled by the Opponent is a sure-fire recipe for feelings of dissatisfaction, anxiety, or depression. In fact, Kabbalah tells us that depression is a direct result of spending too much time thinking of ourselves. If we can remember that our purpose in this life is to reveal the Light, then we can transform our love relationships from "What am I getting?" to "What can I give to this other person?"

Although it didn't happen often I did attend a few parties in high school, but then when I did I usually felt awkward and out of place. Nevertheless, I enjoyed the moments when one of my classmates would tell a joke, or when a few kids would come over and spend five or ten minutes shooting the breeze with me. I remember how their attention—even if brief—made me feel acknowledged and appreciated. During those moments, however brief, I felt included and even, in a small way, important. But as soon as the party was over, the high I'd gotten from those interactions evaporated and my feelings of importance and value went along with it. By the time I returned home, I was often feeling pretty crappy.

What I came to realize was that during these parties I was in reactive mode. I was happy because people were turning their attention toward me, and not because of anything I was generating myself. Since the source of my happiness was external, it was only natural that once I separated myself from that source I would feel a loss of Light and energy. The drug addict from The Centre experienced the same darkness and depression when he ran out of Ecstasy, and that misery is what sent him out chasing another high once again. In the same way, more interactions with the kids from my school could cheer me up again—but since I was merely reacting to their behavior, no matter how positive those interactions might have been the happiness was always short-lived. Eventually I grew tired of my mood swings, and I set out to become the generator of my own happiness.

Of course, we all need interactions with others; connecting to others is essential to our emotional and spiritual growth. But to rely on anyone or anything else to supply us with infinite Light is futile. You can pop a pill, but the effects won't last. You can fall madly in love, but the euphoria will dissipate. You can be swept up in the rush of adrenaline that comes from gambling, or from binging on sweets, or doing drugs, but that, too, will come to an end.

In all of these scenarios, you will be left with one thing: yourself and the reality of the life you have chosen. This is true no matter how hard you try to take yourself out of the present moment and all of the uncomfortable feelings that it sometimes holds. That's because nothing in the physical world lasts forever. Our friends and family can offer us love and support, but when we expect them to be the source of our fulfillment we're setting ourselves up for disappointment—maybe not today, maybe not tomorrow, but it will happen. If we want to experience something more than momentary glimpses of Light, Resistance is the only way.

Examples of revealing the Light through Resistance can be found in every area of our lives. Consider those awe-inspiring images of Earth seen from a satellite. The principle of Resistance is responsible for the startling beauty of our planet, nestled like a sparkling blue-green jewel in the velvety blackness of space. The Earth's atmosphere resists the sun's light, creating illumination. But the void of space produces no Resistance whatsoever, so what we see in the background is darkness. When we listen to our favorite music, the resistance of the guitar strings or the lead singer's vocal cords is being overcome and the result is sound waves. Our eardrums, too, resist the sound, allowing us to experience the breathtaking music.

We humans possess the free will necessary to resist reactive impulses and the pleasurable energy that results from them. But remember that the Opponent will stage one heck of a fight in response. The Opponent's voice inside you might argue, "Isn't a little pleasure now and then justified?" My response: "Not if those fleeting moments come at the expense of eternal Light!"

Do you remember the example of the light bulb? Right before the bulb burns out it gives off the brightest light of its life—but that light always ends in darkness. Similarly, lack of Resistance may generate an impressive burst of feel-good energy, but it is inevitably followed by feelings of emptiness. It may not be as exciting, but choosing Resistance leads to a steady source of Light in our lives. Now that we know the alternative, why would we ever choose darkness over Light, emptiness over a sense of lasting fulfillment, or sadness over eternal bliss?

- An inability to delay gratification (or a failure to apply Resistance) results in a direct connection between you and the Light. This produces an immense spark, but one that immediately fades.

- Temporary highs can be addictive. These addictions can take many forms, including drugs, alcohol, cigarettes, love, sex, food, gambling, relationships, and drama.

- When we choose instant gratification, we recreate the arrangement that existed in the Endless World between the Light and the Vessel. Whatever we are addicted to becomes the Cause, and we become the Effect.

- In order to keep our path continuously illuminated with Light, we need to apply Resistance.

Learning to resist your desire takes time and practice, so don't be upset or ashamed by the times you forget to resist—or simply chose not to. Instead, make a mental note of them. As long as you are working to raise your awareness of your behavior, your actions will naturally begin to change. Take the time right now to write about some recent situations in which your reactive behavior left you feeling high. The rush you felt could have been one of pleasure or one of frustration or anger. Describe how the high felt. Be specific. How long did it last? Seconds, minutes, hours, perhaps days? How did you feel after the rush subsided? Better or worse than before?

# embracing obstacles

**W**e go through our lives doing everything in our power to avoid unnecessary obstacles. But what if we've gotten it all wrong? Instead of trying to break free from life's challenges and hurdles, what if we should actually be *embracing* those that come our way? It's an interesting notion, isn't it? And if it were true, we might start seeing our lives in a whole new light.

Well, what if I told you that it *is* true? Although the Opponent is responsible for the obstacles that appear in our path, their existence is really a gift. How can this be? Because as we've seen, only by applying Resistance can we access the Light. And without obstacles, we have nothing to resist. So the next time you are confronted with a problem, instead of becoming anxious or angry, panicked or preoccupied, pause for a moment and take a closer look at the situation at hand. I guarantee you that it is an opportunity for growth in disguise.

As you'll recall, we spend most of our time in the 1 Percent Realm, which is full of fear and chaos. But beyond the physical world lies the infinitely rewarding 99 Percent Realm, which we are learning to tap into. The true desires of our heart—lasting love, peace of mind, security, well-being—do not exist in the physical realm. They simply can't flourish in a limited, finite space. Therefore, to achieve this lasting fulfillment, we need to connect to the 99 Percent Realm consistently, continuously, and without hesitation.

Obstacles offer us a way to do this. In fact, an obstacle allows Light to come into our lives indirectly, in an indirect manner, which means that we can safely interact with it without fear of burnout. When we put forth the effort and work through an obstacle (by practicing Resistance), we are rewarded with the peace and clarity that only the Light can provide. So, consider obstacles to be blessings! You heard me—blessings!

Granted, this new perspective is going to take some getting used to. There will be times when this notion seems positively ludicrous, and you'll want to shut the book on Kabbalah. And I strongly encourage you to notice this reaction. Recognize your desire to shut down or run away. You can even choose to act on your desire, but you will no longer be able to do so in ignorance. You know too much now. You know that to avoid challenge is to turn away from the Light. And that's definitely not what you're after!

Obstacles or no obstacles, most of us want what we want exactly when we want it. But we might not always be prepared to handle what we think we want. One of the kids I went to school with was incredibly wealthy—or at least his parents were. For months before he turned 16, he began petitioning his parents for a Porsche. He drove everyone crazy bragging about the sports car he was sure to get. Bear in mind, he didn't even have his learner's permit yet! I remember my brother saying to me, "If his parents give him that car, they might as well give him a death sentence while they're at it." Fortunately, the boy's parents were as sensible as they were wealthy. Instead of a sporty little European car for his birthday, they enrolled him in a semester-long driver's ed class. If he wanted to practice driving, he had to do so in his parents' old Cadillac and with his dad in the seat next to him.

Many months later, after he had earned his driver's license, the boy's parents still didn't buy him his dream car—although they had enough money to give him one every year for the rest of his life. Instead they bought him an old, safe, reliable Volvo. They patiently stood back as he learned to take care of his car and drive it responsibly. When the boy finally graduated from college, I heard that he finally received the Porsche he had wanted for so long. By that time, he could fully appreciate the gift and the car, and I'm sure it was well worth the wait!

Even back then, I could see that these were two very wise parents. The Creator "parents" us in the same way. For instance, we may long to meet the man or woman of our dreams, yet it's just not happening. But what if we are simply too young or not yet mature enough to nurture such a relationship? If this is the case, the Light may send us a relationship right now that is full of challenges—opportunities for growth—that will help us develop so that we are fully prepared to meet our soul mate. The obstacles in our path give us a chance to earn the very thing that we so intensely desire.

It's important to understand, too, that different obstacles trigger different reactions in people. We might be able to confront one particular challenge head-on, while another leaves us shaking in our boots or sticking our heads in the sand. In my case, giving a presentation to a room full of people makes me very uncomfortable. For someone else, taking center stage might be a blast. Boarding an airplane is the absolute limit for one good friend of mine. For someone else, it may be confronting a friend who they feel has wronged them in some way. What produces fear or hope in some people is not what produces it in others. When we begin to recognize our limits, we are also taking the first step in overcoming them.

When I was a kid, there was a video game called Pitfall. Start the game and you are immediately dodging holes, rolling barrels, and scorpions. This is not unlike the spiritual path. The moment you begin, you face pitfalls. One of them is confusing Resistance with suppressing your feelings. What's the difference? Suppression has nothing to do with viewing your reactive behavior honestly. In fact, suppression means not viewing your behavior at all! Instead, you just stuff it down. You ignore it.

This reminds me of my own behavior when I was in junior high. There was a boy in my science class who always copied the answers off my tests and assignments. From across the aisle, I could feel his eyes scanning my paper, and this unnerved me. I thought to myself, *while I was at home studying my brains out, this guy was out partying with the popular kids!* Whether or not it was true, this thought left me feeling even more outraged, if that were possible. His behavior really pushed my reactive buttons, but I vowed to myself that I wouldn't respond!

By that time, I had begun to study Kabbalah with my father. I soon realized that I was confusing suppression and Resistance. I thought that by not saying anything to my classmate, I was taking the high road. I honestly thought I was applying the Transformation Formula—but instead of feeling any sense of relief (or Light for that matter), the situation grew steadily worse. My irritation festered, and soon I grew to detest this boy. To make matters more frustrating, he was one of the kids who would occasionally talk to me in between classes or say "Hi" to me in the hall. Instead of helping, though, these seemingly kind gestures just added salt to the wound.

One day, he was straining so hard to copy my answers on a midterm that I could feel his breath on my neck. That was it. I turned to him and shouted, *Stop copying from me! Stop taking everything from me!* His jaw hit the floor, and everyone else in class was just as shocked. Needless to say, that moment ranks up there as one of my most humiliating, but what a lesson I learned! I had confused suppression with Resistance, and the consequences were not pretty. Had I resisted my reactive behavior, I might have chosen to talk to this boy outside of school, or at our lockers after class, or any other time when my emotions weren't boiling over. Perhaps I would have learned that the boy wasn't out having the time of his life every night. In fact, I later discovered that his grandfather was terminally ill and was currently living at his house so the family could care for him. Study time had taken a backseat in his life, and justifiably so.

Resisting our reactions doesn't mean that we allow people to take advantage of us. If my classmate's behavior was making me feel uncomfortable, then it was up to me to find an appropriate solution. By taking the time to seek him out and discuss the situation, I could have gained some much-needed perspective and maybe even found ways in which I could help—and by lending a hand, I would have been accessing even more of the Light of the Creator. Who knows? The whole situation might have led to an amazing friendship. But I didn't do these things, and I couldn't change the past. But I did pick myself up off the floor of shame and set about becoming the Cause—and not the Effect—of my surroundings. Uncomfortable situations will always be with us; this is a fact of life. But responding to them reactively is a choice we don't have to make.

Like suppression, coping is another mechanism that is easy to confuse with Resistance. Coping might be a step up from suppressing, but it's still far from ideal. When you are coping with a person or situation, you have acknowledged the reality of the situation—at least to some degree. But just "getting by" is not what we are after, either. We want change, and coping rarely leads to change. Only by applying Resistance with the intention of converting obstacles into Light can we deal with the Cause of the problem.

Aaron, a friend of mine in junior high, had a younger sister who was battling an eating disorder. We didn't know what that really meant at the time, but we couldn't help but notice that she was unnaturally thin. Aaron's mother walked her two kids to school each morning, dropping Aaron off at our school first and then walking his sister to her school a couple of blocks away. Amy seemed thinner every time we saw her, and when summer arrived, we could see bony knees and elbows poking out of her short-sleeve shirts and shorts. She seemed unhappy most of the time, although every once in a while she would laugh at one of our lame junior high jokes, and it made me feel good to see her enjoying herself for a moment.

During school field trips, we would sometimes partner with Amy's school. We would wander down museum halls together and eat side by side in the lunchrooms. One time Amy finished her meal and got up to use the bathroom. As she did, I heard some of the girls say, "I don't understand the point of being bulimic. Why does she even bother eating in the first place?"

This was the first time I had heard this word *bulimic* used to describe someone I knew personally. Thankfully, when I saw Amy again, things had taken a turn for the better. She was seeing a therapist, and the results showed—both in her appearance and in the way she held herself. Instead of avoiding eye contact and wearing a frown most of the time, she cracked jokes and smiled more often. She seemed to enjoy being around people more, and spoke to me and my friends with more confidence than I'd ever seen in her.

One day, during a school field trip, Amy met my mother, who was a volunteer chaperone. Perhaps because of her own personal struggles, Amy was more interested and receptive to the teachings of Kabbalah than most kids her age. She told my mother that although she was coping with her disorder, she didn't feel truly alive.

Thanks to the heart-felt talk she had with my mom that day, Amy began visiting The Centre regularly and even joined us for dinner some nights. In the beginning, it was difficult for her to share meals with us and even more challenging still to remain sitting at the table. But after several months, it was apparent that she was becoming at ease with our family and with her own body. She returned to a normal weight, and by the time she began high school, Amy was doing volunteer work helping other young women struggling with eating disorders. She told my mom that she was finally able to quiet the negative self-talk that had propelled her into her eating disorder, and that as a result her life was filled with more joy than ever before. Rather than just coping with her situation, Amy went to the root of her problems and, as a result, her life was transformed.

Imagine going on a camping trip. For the first two days you get eaten alive by mosquitoes. You use tons of bug repellant on yourself, but you are still getting bitten. Then one day you notice that your campsite is right next to a large pond of standing water, the ideal breeding ground for mosquitoes. When you pack up your tent and move to a new campsite with a good breeze and no pond nearby, you notice that the mosquitoes are no longer biting you. Actually, there are no mosquitoes at all in your new campsite. You uncovered the root of the problem—the standing water—and you took proactive steps to keep from becoming breakfast, lunch, and dinner for some mosquito. We must be willing to dig deep and unearth the seed of our problems before we will ever experience full recovery from their effects.

Spiritual transformation does not mean just thinking happy thoughts and hoping everything will all work out. On the contrary, transformation is about being willing to face head on whatever life dishes out. Sure, we could meditate on a mountain top, travel to some remote island in the Pacific, or join a convent or cloister and feel temporarily relieved. But escaping life's problems will never result in long-lasting fulfillment—only overcoming obstacles, one at a time, will.

- Satan (the ego) places obstacles along our path. These obstacles, however, are gifts in disguise, because they allow us to practice Resistance and reveal Light.

- Obstacles help us access the Light indirectly, so that we don't burn out like we would if we connected directly with the Light.

- Obstacles help us grow, and prepare us to receive our true desires when the time is right.

- Suppression and Resistance are not the same. Stuffing down our emotions and reactions only delays an inevitable outburst.

- Coping with a situation also fails to uproot the seed of our problem. Only Resistance can bring about root level transformation.

Reflect on a recent argument you may have had with a friend or family member. Was it an outright fight or a more subtle difference of opinion? Write down the circumstances surrounding the disagreement. Did the person involved want you to do something that you didn't want to do, or vice versa? Was there a conflict of interest, or a different recollection of events? How did you respond? Did you suppress or ignore your emotions? Or did you allow yourself to feel them? If you acknowledged your feelings, what did you do next? If you suppressed them, how did that make you feel, and what was the result? Would you say that you coped with the situation, acted reactively, or reacted proactively? What are some ways you might change your response should a similar situation arise in the future? I know that analyzing a painful argument can be difficult, but by looking at our behavior closely we can work to change it if needed. By doing our due diligence now, we bring ourselves closer to the eternal warmth and glow of the Light.

# bigger obstacles = bigger light

loved bagels as a kid (and I still do). Once a week during lunch hour, I'd make the quick dash to the deli across from my high school to pick up my favorite bagel: onion with a thick layer of cream cheese. I can almost taste it now!

Those bagels weren't just your run-of-the-mill prepackaged variety that you pick up in the store these days. They were brought in fresh twice a day and our school break corresponded almost perfectly with the second delivery. Equally as memorable as the bagel was the fact that most of the guys who worked there knew me, and they knew just how I liked my bagel prepared. With them, I never had to wait in line to place my order. This small but significant gesture always made me feel like I belonged and I craved that in high school even more than I craved onion bagels with cream cheese.

But there was this one guy—an older man, with thick sideburns and bushy eyebrows—who made me place my order every time. While the other counter guys might ask me how life was treating me, this man rarely spoke to me at all. And despite my asking for just a dab of cream cheese every time, he would load my bagel with enough cream cheese for a dozen bagels.

At first I would scrape off the cream cheese outside the deli, just to be polite. But as time went on and he continually ignored my request, I began to scrape it off right in front of him, hoping he'd get the message. I never confronted him directly but I figured I was making myself perfectly clear with my obvious display. But the man never indicated that he was getting the hint.

As I scraped my bagel free from its burden of too much cream cheese, I observed my nemesis interacting with other customers. Sometimes he was as terse with them as he was with me, but just as often he would ask someone about their children or spouse or crack a joke. I couldn't help but take this man's behavior personally. After all, the other guys who worked there seemed to like me. I just couldn't figure this guy out, so I started to go to the deli more frequently—even when my mom had packed a perfectly suitable lunch. My mission in life became to get him to pay attention to my order, and to me. During the course of my mission, however, my resentment towards him grew and grew, as I realized that he was not changing in the slightest.

Fortunately, I was focusing on the Transformation Formula in my Kabbalah studies, and the lesson I had learned from my classmate copying my answers was still pretty fresh in my mind. So I decided to practice Resistance, even though I wasn't sure exactly what that implied in this case. Did it mean that I should give up my lunch bagels entirely? Should I find another deli, even though there weren't any others right nearby? Plus, these were my favorite bagels!

None of these solutions felt right, so I decided to continue to go to the deli—on days I was honestly in the mood for a bagel—and to order from whoever was available, but to stop scraping the cream cheese off my bagel in front of this man. Then a strange thing happened. I began to *like* my bagel with extra cream cheese. Not every day, but on the days this man made my bagel, the extra cream cheese became a special treat. When he served me, I stopped requesting less cream cheese. I received exactly the same bagel from him that I always had, but I was no longer setting up an obstacle to enjoying the bagel. I was no longer playing the victim, and taking this man's actions personally. And as a direct result, my life—as it related to situations involving bagels, anyway—became easier!

When the time was right, I experimented again with politely requesting less cream cheese. I explained that the bagel tasted good both ways, but I preferred more bagel and less cheese. He listened, nodded his head, and then said, "I'll remember that next time. Thanks for letting me know." And he did, but I have to admit that from that day forward, I missed the cream cheese with just a hint of bagel that he used to serve me! But I had gained powerful insight into how a tweak in my attitude and interactions with another person could increase my enjoyment of a situation—and a bagel!

This whole ordeal may sound like small potatoes—after all, it didn't deal with addiction, eating disorders, family violence, or the like—but for me it was a real turning point. It showed me, in practical and personal terms, how resisting my instinctual responses could reveal Light in my life. Despite all the time I spent analyzing him, I never learned exactly why the man behaved the way he did. So I stopped trying so hard to figure him out, realizing that sometimes there's just no way of knowing what makes someone else tick. It's hard enough to know our own minds!

Thanks to this situation and others like it, I began to notice that whenever I faced a truly difficult challenge, my urge to react grew right along with it. And the bigger my potential reaction, the more Resistance I needed to apply. And the more Resistance I applied, the more Light that flowed into my life. It was becoming hard to argue with the fact that my life was becoming increasingly richer, the more I trained my mind to respond with openness and compassion to the Opponent's provocations. If every obstacle could be turned into Light, the possibilities for me to feel joy began to seem endless.

I was able to apply the lessons that I learned from the bagel debacle to the basketball coach who refused to let me play varsity, to the girl who declined to go on a date with me, to my biology lab partner who made me do the majority of the work, to my brother, who borrowed my favorite sweatshirt without asking me and then lost it, and to my parents, who, despite the best of intentions, had made my life difficult by carving out a path so unlike anyone else's.

There were times when I was so angry with these people that I could have broken a baseball bat over my knee, and moments when I felt so dejected I could have wept for days. Then there were times when I was so ecstatically happy, I could hardly contain myself. In each case I battled for control over my reactive behavior, while reminding myself that other people's actions usually had nothing to do with me—and even if they did, it didn't mean I had to react to them one way or the other. Instead I learned to experience the present moment just as it was, without having to run in fear from it. This detachment from other people's reactions left a lot more energy, time, and room for happiness in my life.

Learning to sit with the present moment is the start of real change. When we remove ourselves from the present moment with reactive behavior, we remove ourselves from the possibility of transformation. To truly transform we must be open to having a compassionate relationship with all parts of ourselves, even those parts that bring us pain and suffering, and those parts we detest the most. How can we get to know these aspects of ourselves when we are always trying to escape them? If we rein in our reactive behaviors, then we give ourselves room to become acquainted with these reactive traits so that we can then transform them into proactive ones. But we can only do that when we bring them out of the darkness and into the light of day.

This is how it was for me and my Attention Deficit Disorder. Once I stopped beating myself up for not being like everyone else, I was able to get to know this other aspect of myself—an aspect that was ripe with Light-giving potential. This allowed me to stop judging myself, which allowed me to move beyond frustration into a whole new appreciation of my ADD. Even now, I encounter situations on a daily basis in which it is clear to me that my ADD is a gift. It forever reminds me to never judge others, because I don't know the full story behind their actions.

In practical terms, learning to resist reactive behavior is like learning any new skill. It takes practice, and you have to start small. It doesn't make sense to wake up tomorrow morning and decide to start resisting your biggest, most painful reactive behavior. You will need to build up to this. So practice with the guy who never allows you enough room to get into your locker, or the girl who blatantly interrupts you while you are talking. See how it goes. My guess is that it'll go smoother than you imagined. If it doesn't, you will learn from that, too. When you're comfortable, gradually move up to dealing with folks with whom you have more intimate relationships, such as best friends or family members. These people love you unconditionally anyway, so even if your words or actions don't come out perfect, their Light and love will still be with you.

It's some time now since I was a teenager, but I work with many teenagers and I remember how challenging those times were for me. It felt like there were always so many decisions to weigh, and expectations to meet. There was so much of who I was that I did not understand or like. So much of the time things felt flat-out overwhelming, and if I had to guess I would say that being a teenager today is probably even more overwhelming than it was in my time.

It's not always clear which situations require Resistance and which don't. When this happens, we can always remember to tune into our instincts. Pay special attention to those cases when you know something is hurtful to yourself or another person but you decide to do it anyway—or when you get a funny feeling in your stomach that lets you know that something is out of whack.

It's easy to forget that reactive behavior can revolve around seemingly positive interactions, too. Who doesn't like praise, right? But depending on compliments from others can lead us down the same path as any other type of reactive behavior, because we are still reacting to an external stimulus—in this case, someone else's view of us. So as you practice Resistance, be sure to use it with compliments as well as insults! We don't need praise to experience the Light. In fact, the Light is absolutely all we need.

Receiving attention from others can become a confusing matter, especially as it relates to sex. A girl who we'll call Amy had just started dating her first boyfriend, when he started pressuring her to have sex in his car on the drive to and from school. On a gut level, this didn't feel right to her; it was too soon in the relationship—not to mention, it lacked any hint of love or romance.

But he would lay on the charm and Amy didn't want to disappoint him, so she gave in to his advances time and time again. This behavior went on for awhile, until her grades began to drop, she began fighting more with her parents, and her friends complained that they never saw her. Finally she got honest with herself. She wasn't ready for sex, but, at the same time, she liked her boyfriend and didn't want to lose him.

For the first time, Amy came to the realization that every time she had sex, she was being reactive. She was responding to her boyfriend's expectations of her, and by doing so she was closing herself off to the Light. But she was ready to turn things around. Using what she had learned from Kabbalah, Amy was able to rethink her relationship with her boyfriend and come to the conclusion that the next time he made a sexual advance, she would resist. If he broke up with her because of it, then that's how it would have to be. Her integrity and sense of well-being were on the line.

When Amy's boyfriend drove her to school the next day, he parked as usual across from the school building. Then he began making his usual moves. When his hand made its way up her skirt, she removed it. His response was first surprise and then anger. Pouting, he started the car and dropped her off. The next day went the same way. Day after day, his frustration only increased, but she made sure not to respond reactively. Instead, she told him clearly that while she enjoyed kissing and touching him, having sex was not making her happy and she wanted to wait—at least until their relationship matured.

Finally, several weeks after an agonizing breakup, Amy's boyfriend came over to the house and apologized to her. He said he realized what a difficult situation he had put her in, and told her that he admired her courage in standing firm for what she believed. He asked if she would consider dating him again if they took things more slowly. After thinking it over, she agreed, and the last I heard they were still together, long after their rocky beginning.

Happily ever after is always a nice ending to a story, but practicing Resistance rarely ends with two people living together in perfect harmony. Still, when you become willing to let go of unhealthy situations and outcomes, your true desires have a way of becoming fulfilled, although perhaps not exactly as you'd originally imagined. For instance, when Amy resisted she might have lost her boyfriend for good, even if he had eventually changed his mind—but by being single again, she might have opened herself up to meet someone who was more in sync with her desires and values. We have no way of predicting how exactly the Light will come to us, but we do know that it will find us if we make the decision to resist.

With its false promise of freedom from suffering, the path of least resistance can be very enticing, no doubt about it. It fools us with false promises of protection and freedom from suffering. But in the end this course only leaves us more fearful and alienated. It reinforces our sense of being separate, which can be just as effective at keeping out the Light as blackout shades across a window. It restricts our ability to care for ourselves and for others, even those closest to us. Ironically, the more we try to safeguard ourselves from discomfort, the more we inevitably suffer. The Light can't flourish inside the confines of a self-imposed comfort zone. One of the messages of this book is that it's time to leave your comfort zone and welcome—yes, welcome—uncomfortable situations. By doing so, you are also welcoming unlimited fulfillment and infinite joy into your life—which is right where they belong.

Let's say God offered you $100,000 every time someone hurt your feelings, or made you mad—provided that you completely let go of any reactive behavior. Chances are you would be waking up every morning praying for people to hurt you. And when they did, you would practice the Transformation Formula with all your might in order to win the cash prize. Most of us would bend over backwards at a chance like this, and we're only talking about something as impermanent as money. But what if we were talking about the ultimate prize— infinite fulfillment? In fact, that is exactly what we *are* talking about, because God offers you this extraordinary deal every second of your life. Why don't you start taking him up on it? You have nothing to lose and everything to gain.

- Most of the time, people's words and actions have little to do with us. And even if they do, it's up to us to resist the temptation to respond reactively.

- Every person and situation in our lives is a gift— whether it seems that way or not. Everything happens for a reason.

- The more we curb our reactive behavior, the more our lives are filled with the Light.

- Learning to stay in the present moment is the beginning of spiritual transformation.

- In order to experience everything that the Light has to offer, we have to step out of our comfort zones and walk the path of most Resistance.

- Our biggest obstacles reveal the most Light.

Make a list of the last three situations in which you had a strong reaction to an event or a person. If you have been practicing the Transformation Formula, include those experiences as well, even if they weren't entirely success-ful. Next, list your reactions (whether you acted on them or resisted them) in order of intensity. Did you have your biggest reactions to the most emotionally charged situa-tions and your smallest reactions to the least overwhelm-ing situations?

Consider the amount of Light you could potentially let into your life by resisting these reactions. Now make a list of situations in which you habitually respond reactively. Your teammate gets a better time than you on the 100 meter dash. A girl in your class flirts with you. You fail to study for a quiz. You smoke pot when it is offered to you. It does-n't matter if the situations are seemingly positive or nega-tive, if you have a typical reaction to it, list the situation.

Now rate them in order of how much emotion your reaction contains, from a low of 1 to a high of 10. Now, start with the lower numbers (1, 2, and 3) and challenge yourself to resist your reactive behavior to these people or situations until you experience a natural shift in your response. Then move up the list until you are tackling your nines and tens. Adjust the list as your life changes. Remember, your life will only get better as you grow more willing to tackle the hard stuff.

# certainty is the answer to every challenge

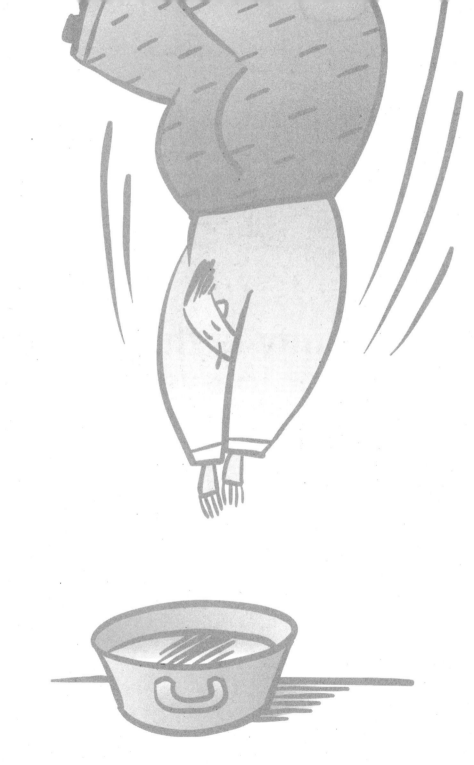

**N**o one enters this world free of spiritual baggage, according to Kabbalah. This baggage—accumulated over many prior lifetimes—is made up of all the times our reactive behavior got the best of us. But along with this baggage comes some important news—at some time during our life or lifetimes, we will be given an opportunity to correct our behavior. This concept of correction is called *"tikkun"* and it is the heart of our spiritual work.

We know we have stumbled across our personal *tikkun* when a situation makes us squirm in our shoes! Maybe we find managing money a challenge, or perhaps we are easily intimidated by authority figures, or by those whom we feel have more popularity or power. Perhaps we struggle with weight, or body image. If so, we are standing face to face with our personal *tikkun*—that aspect of ourselves that cries out for correction. If we find it difficult to tell our teacher that we think she graded our essay unfairly, or if it practically kills us to introduce ourselves to someone new, then we are encountering a future correction in the works.

If this concept still feels a little fuzzy, start by looking for repetitive behavior. If you always seem to work hard but can't seem to make the grade, while your friend slacks off and gets A's every time, that's a *tikkun*. And if you always find yourself attracted to the same type of friends or significant others, you guessed it— *tikkun*! If it is a struggle, it is a *tikkun*.

Unfortunately, when we fail to resist a reactive behavior it becomes more difficult to correct the next time around. It's like eating ice cream one night, so the next night you find yourself craving it again at about the same time. Before you know it, every night you're eating ice cream before bed and a new dependence on sweets has taken root. The more we feed a reactive trait, the stronger it grows. And the Opponent bulks up, too, right along with it. As a result, our *tikkun* will appear over and over again, through various people and situations.

Initially we may not even recognize the correction in its various forms. For instance, your weakness in dealing with aggressive people might show up today in the form of the driver full of road rage in the lane next to you, and tomorrow as an irritated waiter who feels you slighted him on the tip. But the more you test the wisdom in this book, the easier it will become to identify a particular *tikkun*. If you are in a situation that is making you uncomfortable, then you can be fairly certain you are facing a *tikkun*. And how do we fix a *tikkun*? Through Resistance, of course!

If you want to see an entertaining depiction of the kabbalistic principle of *tikkun*, check out *Groundhog Day*. In this film, Bill Murray plays Phil Connors, a weatherman who is the ultimate reactive character—self-consumed, ego-driven, and oblivious to the feelings of others. But his life turns upside down when he gets stuck in a time warp on February 2. He keeps re-living this day, Groundhog Day, over and over again, but no one knows this but him.

It is fun at first, as Phil takes advantage of the situation and learns to manipulate everyone in his life to serve his own self-interests. But the joke is on him as his life slowly turns into a nightmare. Phil awakens every morning to the same day and the same momentary pleasures, but there is not an ounce of lasting fulfillment in the life he has chosen. There is no escape—not even death.

Finally, Phil takes matters into his own hands. He decides to change himself, since it has become obvious that he cannot change the world around him. He begins to perform good deeds and helps people who are encountering the same misfortunes day after day. And, as you might have guessed, these small acts of kindness lead him to experience true joy for the first time in his life. Inspired by the Light he is experiencing, he goes on a sharing "binge" all over town, winning the hearts of everyone. Eventually, his hard work pays off as he awakens to a brand-new day, in the arms of the woman of his dreams. Sure, it's a movie, but *Groundhog Day* has a message that also holds true in the real world: If we want to put an end to a life that feels like a repetitive nightmare, then we have to put an end to our own reactive behavior.

Like Phil's life in *Groundhog Day*, there are certain reoccurring patterns that appear in everyone's life. These patterns are our *tikkun*, and our mission is to practice Resistance in order to make the necessary correction to that *tikkun*. Let's take a closer look at this process. The following are some patterns that many people experience in their own lives. Observe whether any of them pertain to you.

### Resisting Laziness

You have a chemistry quiz tomorrow morning that you haven't studied for, even though your teacher gave you a review sheet that practically spells out what will be on the quiz. You have plenty of time to sit down and work through a few problems, but your favorite show is on television. Then it's time for dinner, and after that there's more television to watch. Sound familiar? If it does, your *tikkun* may be procrastination and idleness. Resistance doesn't necessarily imply stopping something else, or standing still. Often it means overcoming the desire to do nothing and diving in headfirst.

### Resisting Ego

You and your classmates have just finished your first day of an intro to web design class, and everyone is talking about their ideas for the first assignment. The class was a little boring for you since you have already designed your own website and have even helped a few friends with theirs. You feel an urge to show off your knowledge, but you recognize that this is your ego at work. Still, this desire to show people how smart you are is a habit with you. Your *tikkun* may be a feeling of superiority, so resist it by not saying a word. Recognize the spiritual opportunity and let it go. The Light will enter, and you may even learn something valuable from the conversation.

## Resisting Judgment

Your friend calls you to complain about another friend of yours. As she fills you in on her side of the story, you can't help but think that the story *is* pretty appalling! Based on what your friend on the phone has described to you, you are ready to pass judgment and choose sides. Resist! Let go of your emotions. Wait for your other friend to tell you his side before coming to a conclusion. Your *tikkun* is probably connected to judgmental behavior, and you need to learn that there are two sides to every story.

## Resisting Self-Involvement

All but one of the colleges you applied to have sent you acceptance letters, and you can't make up your mind which one to attend. You run through lists of the pros and cons. You ask your mother for advice. Then your father. Then your brother, even though he's just finishing the third grade. You're spending your evenings on the internet reading every last review, opinion, and assessment of your potential schools. When you're not on the computer, you are on the phone getting feedback from friends. Everyone has different advice, soon you're a bundle of stress and you're no closer to a decision.

Resist the urge to wallow in your indecision. Go out and do something good for someone else. Spend a little time helping others with their issues. When you get out of your own way, answers will come to you when you least expect them.

## Resisting Evil Impulses

What a lousy day! You got an F on your Geometry mid-term, and your parents took away your internet rights as punishment. You're feeling extremely irritable. Then a friend calls, and after a bit of small talk, begins bad-mouthing a girl you both know. You join in. Hearing about someone else's troubles makes you feel better about your own lousy day. But resist the desire to gossip and speak badly of others! Kabbalistically, the sin of murder is not limited to physical death; it also includes character assassination. When we speak unkindly of our friends, we are killing their value in the eyes of another person. Getting off of the phone or changing the subject is therefore the equivalent of saving someone's life. This will reveal tremendous Light, which is what you really need in order to feel better about your situation.

## Resisting Control

You've been writing poetry for years. When you hear about a poetry open-mike night at a local café, you decide to give it a try. You are nervous as can be, and after hearing some of the other poets, you decide you just don't have what it takes. You decide to pack up your things and take your latte to the back door. Resist! You are not the source of your poetry; the Light is responsible for all works of art. Great writers know that they are just channels. So give up control. Let go of your personal attachment to your work, take the stage, and read your message. The Light will take care of the rest.

## Resisting Expectations

- Your friend vowed to do anything for you after you helped him prepare for his math final, but when you ask him to help you change the oil in your car, he claims he has another commitment.
- You can't wait to go on spring break with your classmates. The forecast calls for nothing but blue sky and sunshine, but it rains in torrents for the first three days of your trip.
- You have started getting high after school with the cool kids. You expect them to be nicer to you now when you see them in the halls, but they still don't acknowledge you.

Resist all your feelings of disappointment! And put the brakes on that sense of victimization you feel. Something better is on its way. Try embracing the kabbalistic principle of asking the Light for what you need in life, not what you want. Later, you will see the hidden blessing in what feels like such a let-down now.

### Resisting Lack of Confidence

You've been selected by your orchestra teacher to give a cello solo at the year-end concert. Your natural reaction is, "I can't do it; I'm not good enough. I don't want all that attention focused on me." This is reverse ego at work, but it is still ego. It's time to let go of your limited thinking. It's not all about you; other people are involved, and there is a bigger picture to be seen. Focus on thinking of your performance as a way of sharing with the audience so they can have an enjoyable evening, and you'll find yourself effortlessly making beautiful music.

### Resisting Insecurity

You have been invited to a dance or social event, and you are excited, but you have no idea what you should wear. For weeks you fret about what the other people might be wearing, what they'll think of what you are wearing, and whether you'll measure up in comparison. You hate these types of functions for this very reason—you simply don't feel comfortable. Maybe you should back out and avoid this nonsense entirely. After all, you'll feel better at home in some comfortable sweatpants and a remote control in your hand.

But you'll never grow if you don't confront your issues. Resist the temptation to hide, and more importantly, resist playing the comparison game. Trust me, you'll never win; no one wins that game except Satan. Instead, wear something you feel good in, and go out and enjoy yourself, and realize that it is never about anyone else—it's about connecting to the Light, about being a channel for Light!

### Resisting Embarrassment

In the middle of band practice, the teacher waves her hands for the music to stop. Everyone sees her but you. You continue playing your instrument for an extra two bars, until you realize that everyone is staring at you—but it's not because they are in awe of your gifted music-making. You turn deep red and pray, as you try desperately to hide your embarrassment that the floor swallows you up.

Resist! Embrace the humiliation. Take it all in. Lower your defenses, and soak up as much embarrassment as possible. By making yourself vulnerable and by remembering that you are human, you keep the ego in check. In the grand scheme of things your mistake doesn't even register. In a day or two no one will even remember it; or if they do, it's because it was a funny moment that people got a kick out of. That's how the Light works.

## Resisting the Need to Be Admired

You're at a party with school friends, and you're meeting kids from another school. You're introduced as the "funny one" in your group, so now you feel pressure to crack jokes just so you can prove them right. Resist! Just say, "I have been known to make a joke or two," and leave it at that. Resist the temptation to become the evening's entertainment. While you're at it, resist those reactive thoughts that are telling you that your friends may not like, admire, or look up to you any more if you fail to deliver.

## Resisting Doubts

You apply the wisdom of Kabbalah and the principle of Resistance to a real-life situation with your friend or parent, but the results are nil. Your mind is flooded with doubts. *It doesn't work*, you say to yourself. Resist these reactive thoughts! This is just a test to see if you've truly surrendered. Whenever you become attached to an outcome, you're missing the point of the exercise. That's the paradox: Look for results and you won't see them. Stop looking and you'll get it all!

At the heart of each of these scenarios is a feeling of uncertainty, a sense that running from what we fear would be better than trusting that our needs will be provided for. The way to counter this false notion is by injecting certainty into the picture. But what does that mean? Most of you are probably familiar with the story of Moses leading the Israelites out of bondage. Pharaoh and his army had chased the Israelites to the very edge of the Red Sea, where it seemed they were doomed. But despite their fear, Moses led his people into the sea until their noses and ears filled with water. In desperation, Moses called out to God for help, to which God responded, "Why are you calling out to me?"

Moses and his people had no choice but to set aside their fears and continue on into even deeper water. And sure enough, before the water could drown them, the Red Sea parted, allowing Moses and his people to escape without harm.

It's an exciting story. And, according to Kabbalah, it's also code. "Egypt" is a reference to our physical existence in the 1 Percent Realm, while "Pharaoh" is code for the human ego and humanity's reactive and self-seeking nature. In other words, Pharaoh is any aspect of our nature that enslaves or controls us. As for God's enigmatic answer to Moses' plea—*Why are you calling out to me?*—Kabbalah teaches that concealed within this question is a profound spiritual truth: God did not part the Red Sea. In fact, God was surprised that Moses even called upon Him at that moment! Why? Because He knew that Moses and his people had all of the power they needed to part the sea. And they tapped into that power when they chose to relinquish their fear and inject certainty into the equation. We have this same power at our disposal twenty-four hours a day, seven days a week.

Recall the previous scenarios we discussed in this chapter. In addition to uncertainty, they also share the idea of temptation. Like a street dealer selling his wares, the Opponent flashes instant gratification in front of us each time we walk by—and all too often we accept. As we discussed earlier, the burst of Light supplied by instant gratification is intense. In fact, it is usually much brighter than the consistent Light supplied by Resistance. If we forget this for even one moment, we can easily be seduced into doing anything. Drugs, alcohol, and sex are all like light bulbs just before the filament burns through—we receive a flash of bright light, but absolute darkness follows right behind.

David, a popular young man in his teens, began visiting our Centre several years ago. David appeared to have it all. He played several sports and was the captain of the football team. He had a nice girlfriend and caring, involved parents. But despite what appeared to be the perfect life, David saw himself as an outsider looking in. He felt uncomfortable with his own reputation. Plus, he feared that his girlfriend liked him only because his parents were rich.

But his biggest fear was that he would never be able to realize his dream: David wanted to become an artist. He wasn't even sure what kind of artist, because he'd never been given the opportunity to explore his talents—but he liked the idea of moving to a big city after high school, living in a studio with lots of natural sunlight, hanging out at cafés and bars, and creating great art that would make people respect his mind, not just his athletic ability. David had shared his dreams with his girlfriend, his parents, and some of his good friends, but no one took him seriously. Everyone assumed that David would go on to a good college on a football scholarship; after which he would probably take over his dad's business. All David knew to do was continue along meeting everyone else's expectations but his own. But there was a price to pay for living a life that wasn't his own— David felt chronically frustrated and lonely. He felt trapped and misunderstood, incapable of acting on his true needs.

One night at a party, a kid David didn't know well offered him some cocaine. David had smoked pot a couple of times before and hadn't really liked it. He also knew that as an athlete he should steer clear of drugs, but he was tired of doing the right thing. And he was also tired of feeling lousy. So he snorted one line and then another. Sure enough, in no time he felt great. He walked around the party chatting easily with everyone—even the artists and creative types whom he'd always been hesitant to approach.

In the weeks that followed, David did more cocaine. He began buying his own supply rather than relying on others. He also dropped a lot of weight, which pleased David but infuriated his coach. His academic performance fell off a bit, but nothing disastrous. And his girlfriend complained that he was not acting like himself, but she stayed with him anyway.

Cocaine seemed like the perfect drug. When David was high, he felt at ease and self-assured. He could talk to anyone, and the fear that he had been feeling for what seemed like years melted away. But the mornings after a night of doing coke were a struggle. He felt overwhelmed with feelings of grief and despair. Wracked with guilt, he'd lie in bed hoping the world had forgotten about him altogether, but his parents would rouse him up and force him to go to school.

When David couldn't take this morning routine any longer, he found a solution to this problem, too. He discovered that if he did a line or two of coke in the bathroom right when he got out of bed, it would give him the energy he needed to start his day. Not to mention that it helped settle his feelings of worthlessness in the process. After a semester of unreliable and erratic conduct, his football coach booted him off the team, his girlfriend dumped him, and David's parents grounded him for two weeks.

Like any one of us is capable of doing, David had become dependent on an external force—in this case, drugs—to bring him what he believed was some form of inner peace. But looking for an outside solution for an inside job is like putting a band-aid on your head to stop a headache. It'll never work!

Furthermore, although David believed that he was protecting himself from pain and suffering, he was actually adding to his misery by closing himself off from the people who cared about him the most. Sure, getting high felt phenomenal for a few hours. But payback came without fail the morning after, and it was an extremely bitter pill to swallow. So what did David do? He went back for more, thereby sidestepping the reality of his situation once again.

David was finally able to break this vicious cycle and get clean. But the only way to get there was via the path of Resistance. He had to constantly remind himself that what he was giving up was only a fleeting form of pleasure, and what he was receiving in return for his efforts was the lasting joy of the Light. Whenever he felt overwhelmed—which was often—he injected certainty. He decided to let go of his friends' and family's expectations of him—as well as the unhealthy standards he had set for himself. By allowing himself to stay in the moment and experience it fully, he gained the opportunity to feel an entire range of feelings, including sadness and happiness, frustration and excitement. By understanding that one feeling does not overrule another, he was able to let these complex feelings coexist. And by doing so, he let the Light shine in his life.

As a result, David experienced an almost immediate transformation. His parents treated him to a long vacation overseas, and when he returned he met a wonderful girl and fell in love. During his recovery, David had begun to try his hand at ceramics and was accepted to an art school, not on the basis of his athletic abilities but on the merits of his artistic talent. In addition, he began volunteering at a local community center that helped kids to get off drugs. All in all, he felt extraordinarily lucky and fulfilled.

But David fell into a new trap—he became as addicted to praise as he had been to cocaine. An addiction to approval might not have the same type of consequences as a drug addiction, but in both cases, a dependence on external stimuli can wreak havoc on a life. Now it was time for David to practice Resistance on his desire for feedback and approval.

The lesson here is that even after David faced one of his *tikkuns* and transformed it, there was still more work to be done. And there always will be. Be careful not to think that one act of Resistance will fix everything. This process is ongoing; the good news is that you have your whole life to perfect it! Rest assured that as your ability to resist grows stronger, you will notice changes—and miracles—all around you; and most importantly, within you.

It all starts with shutting down thoughts of uncertainty, and embracing certainty in everything you do. Now, keep in mind that injecting certainty does not guarantee that you will always get what you want, but it does ensure that you will always get what you need. For instance, just because you walk around for weeks chanting, "I want a brand-new Prius when I turn sixteen" and being sure that you will get one, doesn't necessarily mean that one will be sitting in your driveway with a big red bow on your birthday. I'm not saying it's not possible; I'm just saying that certainty doesn't always work as you might expect. Like my classmate who wanted a new Porsche but got a Volvo, only the Creator knows precisely what you need to transform your *tikkun*. What you *can* be sure of is that you will be given every tool necessary to turn a less than joyous existence into a life of immense Light and hope.

- We each arrive in this world with spiritual baggage, which is made up of all the times we failed to resist our reactive behavior in the past.

- According to Kabbalah, this baggage is called our *tikkun*, and it is our responsibility to correct and transform our *tikkun* into Light.

- Repetitive and uncomfortable patterns are indications of our *tikkun*.

- Resistance can take many forms. Sometimes it requires a physical action (like turning off the television), while at other times an internal modification is needed (such as a change in our thinking). Becoming aware of our patterns is the first step in practicing Resistance.

- Injecting Certainty into overwhelming situations clears the way for miracles and transformation.

- Certainty does not mean you get what you want; it means trusting that what you get is what you need.

Consider the various Resistance stories you've read. Have you had any similar experiences? Write them down using as much detail as you can. What was your mental and physical response to these situations? Did you overlook any intuitive hunches? List at least two ways in which you could have injected certainty into each situation. Consider what the outcome might have been. Would you have gotten the results you wanted? How about the results you needed? What might the difference have been?

# the power of the
# hebrew letters

One of the kids in my high school was known for his unpredictable hair color. One week he would dye his hair jet black, and the next he would show up with hair the color of the sun. Streaks of hot blue and the occasional pink were not out of his realm either, but the teachers usually threw enough of a fit that he reserved those colors for special occasions. The funny thing was that the kid's natural color was a deep chestnut brown; and it looked good on him, but that didn't matter—he was experimenting, and there didn't seem to be any harm in it. Few people would argue that it was a heck of a lot safer than playing around with drugs or guns, for instance.

My classmate's hair color became a topic of discussion in our household, mostly because I was hoping to persuade my folks to let me color mine, as well. But my dad's take on the situation made me rethink things. He said that the hair dye represented external change and was therefore not unlike all the maneuvering we go through to avoid pain and find happiness. But like the kid's dyed hair that returned to its natural color within a couple of weeks, external changes are also impermanent. My dad reminded me that if we want to make lasting change, we must make it at the seed level. In a human body, that level is our DNA. For example, if my classmate wanted a permanent hair color change, he would have needed a way to alter his DNA. But I don't think permanent hair color was what he was looking for!

As my father and I continued our discussion, he asked me to consider how many times I had attempted to make a change in my behavior only to find myself reverting back to my old ways. I had to admit that this was the case most of the time. Did anyone, I asked him, have the emotional and spiritual strength to permanently stop their reactive behavior dead in its tracks? Or possess the ability to see beyond the present moment to the consequences of their actions? My father's answer was no; no individual possesses such power. Wow, that was disappointing to hear!

What was the point of my practicing Resistance, then, if my DNA would surface again, just like my classmate's roots?

My father reassured me that Kabbalah provided tools that would strike at the deepest level of our existence and would have a lasting impact. Earlier we defined the 99 Percent Realm as the DNA level of our reality, as the Cause of all Causes. Then we discussed the fact that when the Satan came into being, he reconfigured the DNA of the *Desire to Receive* into the *Desire to Receive for the Self Alone*. So we do have a loose working notion about DNA. But what is it, really?

The best way to describe DNA is an instruction manual for our cells. At the very beginning of new life, our cells do not yet have specific jobs. It's up to our DNA to determine which cells will become internal organs, or skin, or bones, or brain matter, or other tissues. Like all instruction manuals, DNA is written in a language that is composed of an alphabet. In this case it's a code—one that was cracked in the late 1950s by geneticists who determined that the DNA alphabet is composed of four "letters," which they designated A, T, C, and G. These letters combine to form "words" and "sentences," which are the genetic code of every individual.

We each have about three billion letters in our genetic codes. The differences between us lie in the combination and sequences of these four letters. And each cell in our body contains the whole three-billion-letter instruction manual. So in a physical sense, all we are is a walking, talking, breathing set of letters!

In truth, the entire universe is alphabetical in nature. Just as letters combine to form words, atoms combine to create more complicated structures known as molecules. Just as words combine to form sentences, molecules combine to create matter—in all its endless forms.

It was only within the last 50 years that scientists uncovered the story of DNA. Abraham, however, described these very concepts some 4000 years ago in *The Book of Formation*. Here Abraham explained that our entire universe consisted of building blocks. Moreover, he said that these building blocks were alphabetical in nature! Abraham went on to reveal how the Light of the Creator had fragmented into 22 distinct forces in order to create our universe. These 22 forces are actually 22 letters.

But according to Kabbalah these aren't your everyday letters. These letters of the Hebrew alphabet existed at the very moment of creation, which makes them vehicles of divine, primordial energy brimming with transformative power. They appear as shapes, but they are much more than the lines and curves that they form—they are energetic vibrations that we can visualize, as well as vocalize. In fact, the Hebrew word for *letter* actually means "pulse," or "vibration."

By virtue of their shapes, sounds, and vibrations, these letters awaken and harness the energy of the universe. Some of the world's most famous scientists, philosophers, mathematicians, and physicians, not to mention many great painters, writers, and musicians utilized the power of the Hebrew alphabet.

A friend of mine, Dr. Artur Spokojny, has also put these letters to the test and experienced profound results. A board-certified internist and cardiologist, Dr. Spokojny studied medicine at Harvard and graduated *summa cum laude* from Düsseldorf University in Germany. Spokojny, who was instrumental in developing laser treatments for heart disease, held a faculty position at Cornell Medical College. I offer you this list of impressive credentials with the hope that you will take seriously the amazing experience I'm about to describe!

One evening a patient who was having a heart attack was rushed into the emergency room. Thankfully, the patient was conscious, but his slow heartbeat was a cause for great concern—in fact, Dr. Spokojny and his team discovered that the patient's right coronary artery was completely blocked. They worked on the man in the operating room for nearly an hour, but hope was wearing thin. Dr. Spokojny later told me that he felt powerless and was at a total loss as to what medical procedure to try next. But at this moment of utter despair, he decided to take another route all together. He chose to meditate on a sequence of Hebrew letters that are known for their healing abilities.

Dr. Spokojny sensed a shift in the energy of the room the moment he began visualizing the letters. Within seconds, the blocked artery cleared, leaving him and his entire team in shock. What had just happened wasn't physically possible—the massive blood clot that had been lodged in the patient's artery should have prevented it from opening. More remarkable still, when the whole ordeal was over, there was no damage whatsoever to the man's heart. It was as though the heart attack had never happened at all.

The patient later told Dr. Spokojny that while the doctors were fighting for his life, he had dreamed he was trapped inside a computer monitor. As he tried desperately to escape, he suddenly found the right sequence of letters for the password. Instantly the doors opened, and he was free.

Later still, Dr. Spokojny discussed the episode with the other doctors involved. They were still scratching their heads in amazement at what happened; their patient should have been dead, but instead he was more alive than ever before. Dr. Spokojny chose to keep his secret to himself, taking no credit for his "last-ditch" effort that produced such life-altering results.

On the books this may remain a medical mystery, but it's no longer a secret that these ancient Hebrew letters are physical and spiritual miracle-workers. They can do for us what we can't do for ourselves, by supplying us with the emotional power and inner strength we need to overcome any obstacle. Moreover, different combinations of letters create different blends of energy, just as different combinations of musical notes create different melodies. The Light they emit clears destructive impulses from our hearts and minds, removing such negative emotions as fear and anxiety. These ancient Hebrew letters can also promote financial abundance, emotional well-being, and physical healing—and that's just the beginning!

If you haven't the faintest notion of how to read Hebrew, have no worries. The power in these letters can be transmitted to us simply by scanning the letters in much the same way that a product scanner reads a bar code. If we want to deepen the experience, we can meditate on the letters, as Dr. Spokojny did. How can these simple acts make such a difference? The answer lies in our eyes. In fact, ancient sages considered the eyes to be the window to the soul. Therefore, visually interacting with these letters in any way connects our souls to the 99 Percent Realm. That's the Cliff Notes answer, anyway.

If you want the deeper answer, it goes like this. The Light of the Creator gave birth to both the human soul, as well as to the infinitely powerful force contained within the Hebrew letters. When the two are in proximity—achieved by visually scanning, meditating, or reciting the letters—a perfect resonance is created, and the energy of the letters is duplicated in the human soul. Yes, this is some very deep and profound stuff, but these letters have remarkably practical applications. When used regularly, they can bring about change in all areas of our life; nothing is beyond their scope and power.

Correcting our reactive behavior is an especially great place to start putting the letters into action, since only by diligently transforming our reactive nature can we return home to the 99 Percent Realm. Thankfully, we don't have to do it without Divine help.

We've been given a set of tools that are as old as time, and these letter tools come in arrangements that are known to kabbalists as the 72 Names of God.

There are three prerequisites to activating the power of the 72 Names:

1. Conviction of their power;
2. An understanding of the particular influence emanating from each Name;
3. A follow-through physical action to activate their power.

The first requirement rests entirely in your ability to ignore the incessant voice of the Opponent, who wants nothing more than to persuade you to disregard the power of these letters. By not reacting to his cynicism, you open yourself up to receive the Light for which you have worked so hard.

As for the second requirement, no action is necessary on your part. After centuries of secrecy, the spiritual influence and power of each Name are now fully accessible to you. Appreciating this fact will further enrich your connection to the Light.

The third requirement is often the most challenging. For example, if you are using a particular Name to conquer your fear of flying, you will have to confront that fear in order to eradicate it from your life. At some point, it will be up to you to board a plane and sit back while it takes flight. It is only by taking this physical step that you "flip the switch," and allow Light to eradicate your fear. If this sounds too daunting, know that when you confront your fear with your newfound spiritual strength, you are certain to conquer it, and by doing so you'll be well on your way to a life free of fear.

Remember the story of Moses and the Israelites? During their exodus, God instructed Moses and his people to "go jump in the water." It was in this moment that the Israelites were being asked to perform the physical act of confronting their fears. Before and during the act of wading into the waters, Moses and the Israelites meditated on sequences from the 72 Names. By meditating, they were expressing their conviction, or injecting certainty into their situation—and by taking action and walking into the treacherous waters, they were activating the mind-blowing power of these 72 Names.

This is significant stuff. What is clear from this story from the Book of Exodus (besides Moses and his people making great role models!) is that God never answers prayers. Instead, God helps us figure out how to answer our own prayers! We do so by learning how to connect to and utilize the Divine energy of the Creator and the Godlike force we all have within us.

Our minds are unable to even imagine the power contained in the Hebrew letters, but that does not make them any less useful or effective. If you are interested in seeing if that power can make a difference in your life, take a look at a book I've written called *The 72 Names of God*. It contains images of the letters themselves, and describes which Hebrew letters to meditate on when you're faced with a specific challenge, whether it's school, or your family, or your love life.

- External changes never last. We must alter our DNA in order to achieve lasting change.

- Only scanning the 72 Names of God gives us the power to change our DNA permanently.

- Scanning the letters connects our souls to the 99 Percent Realm, and everything that the 99 Percent Realm has to offer.

- By meditating on these all-powerful letters, we are able to access the Light of the Creator that has always been within us.

- Circumstances in our life will reappear until we figure out how to transform them into Light.

Make a list of three things that you are afraid of. They can be tangible items (such as big dogs or hairy spiders) or intangible situations (such as a fear that your boyfriend or girlfriend might leave you). Now review the three prerequisites to engaging the power of the 72 Names of God. How strong is your conviction in their power? How might you increase your faith in their transformative abilities? For each of the fears that you wrote down, jot down one or two specific actions you could take that would help to activate the power of the letters. Consider your action items thoughtfully, and resist the temptation to take the easy way out. If you take this exercise seriously, you will be prepared for the moment when you make visual contact with the letters.

exercise:

# the negativity around us is a mirror of our own negative traits

**W**hen I was in junior high school, I knew this kid who always wanted to borrow something from me. His requests always started off with friendly chit-chat. He'd ask me questions about my life in a way that led me to believe he cared, but before the conversation was through he'd invariably ask to borrow a school book or to catch a ride home after school when my mom picked me up. His requests were never-ending, but my patience, on the other hand, was not. After a while, I'd had it. Sure, I enjoyed feeling needed, but this situation was becoming downright ridiculous. Not to mention that the phrase "thank you" seemed to be missing from my classmate's vocabulary.

My annoyance only increased as the days and weeks rolled by. I found myself keeping a mental list of all the ways in which my friend was taking advantage of me. Don't get me wrong—the guy was nice enough, but he was so needy!

About this time, I was becoming increasingly interested in Kabbalah, so if there wasn't basketball practice after school I would spend the rest of my day hanging around The Kabbalah Centre. The visitors and the folks who worked at The Centre all seemed genuinely glad to be there, and I felt comfortable talking to them about whatever was troubling me. I might have felt out of place at school, but I felt at home at The Centre.

One of the people I enjoyed talking to affectionately said to me one day, "Yehuda, you want so much. You are like a great big well that can't be properly filled because you have sprung a leak somewhere deep." As you can imagine, this observation really rubbed me the wrong way. So I began to avoid this man, who to this point had become a mentor to me.

Meanwhile, at school, my friend needed to copy my notes from science lab and, at lunch, he asked to trade the less desirable parts of his lunch for my dessert. Not to mention, he needed me to go to a party with him because the captain of the hockey team would be there. And for some reason, the more he asked of me the harder it was for me to face the man at The Centre! Any connection? Perhaps!

Thanks to my regular Kabbalah study sessions with my dad and brother, the pieces started to fit together. And one day a light bulb went on in my head! I recognized that my classmate's behavior was exactly what I had been exhibiting at The Centre. Even though it had never dawned on me that I was being needy in my interactions there, I had developed an expectation that the people from The Centre would always be there to listen and offer their guidance. No wonder I hadn't been able to face my friend! I had thought I was angry with him, but I was merely attempting to dodge an aspect of myself that I wasn't ready until now to look at.

Admitting to our negative traits is never a walk in the park. It is infinitely easier to spot the faults of others—and complaining about them is even easier! But recognizing those same traits in ourselves can be embarrassing, frustrating, and very painful. This is why we must be extremely gentle with ourselves during this process. Remind yourself that becoming aware of negative traits is not the same as judging them. Judgment is a reactive behavior no matter how you slice it, even when you are applying it to yourself. Instead of judging, gently observe. What do you see?

If you are not yet able to see yourself clearly, then ask yourself: *What are the traits in those around me that bother me the most?* Chances are you exhibit some variation of these traits yourself. This discovery is nothing to be ashamed of. Not at all. In fact, it's cause for celebration! Without obstacles—which is what our negative traits are—we would have nothing to transform and would therefore be cut off from the Light. Owning up to obstacles—taking responsibility for them and applying these steps to them—is challenging. But the alternative is far worse—a lifetime trapped in repetitive, reactive behavior. As Bill Murray's character in *Groundhog Day* discovered, prison would be more comfortable! And it is incredibly beneficial, if not necessary, to have a loving support system while you do this deep spiritual work.

Thankfully, I was able to discuss this eye-opening insight about my recent behavior with my dad. He reminded me that I shouldn't get too attached to locating my negative traits and transforming them. When we do, we give our egos the opportunity to talk us into a spiritual witch-hunt with our own souls as the target. Negative traits are inherent to being human. They should be considered opportunities to transform, not opportunities to berate ourselves and make matters worse.

Negative character traits, as my dad explained, can be compared to a mirror that reflects all of our reactive instincts back at us. Now take this mirror, he said, and imagine it shattering into a million little pieces that float out into the universe. All the negative people, all the negative situations and obstacles that you confront, all the things you see wrong in others, are merely pieces of that mirror. When you transform a particular piece of your reactive character, one of the fragments of the mirror will reflect this change! More and more, you will begin to notice the positive aspects of those around you, and situations in your life that once frustrated you will begin to change for the better, as well.

Perhaps you've heard this before, but it's worth repeating: You can't change another person. That's not to say that you can't provide help on a physical, mental, emotional, or spiritual level; it's not to say that you can't attempt to influence people in ways you think would benefit them; and it's not to say that you can't model positive behaviors and act as a role model. But ultimately you cannot make someone become the way you want them to be. You can't transform someone else's reactive traits for them— not even if you love them more than anything.

Despite this fact, for reasons that vary from genuine kindness to flat-out manipulation, we spend untold amounts of time trying to change everyone from our closest friends to complete strangers (remember the bagel man?). But regardless of our motives, attempting to change another person is a colossal waste of time and energy. Changing ourselves is hard enough! But let's say that you did somehow manage to change another person—you would only be causing them to have Bread of Shame. Why? Because they need to be responsible for their own change. You can't do it for them.

Spending our days and nights trying to change everyone around us is one more way to avoid having to look at our own traits that need changing. This reminds me of a young woman, Jennifer, whom I knew from The Kabbalah Centre. In high school she had begun dating a guy named Aaron. I met him a couple of times, and he seemed like a nice guy. She told me that he was smart, funny, and extremely kind to her. She was crazy about him, and the feeling was mutual.

But Aaron drank too much. If they went to parties together and he drank his usual quota, Jennifer was often scared to ride home with him. In her mind it was even worse when he acted inappropriately in public, like when he groped her in front of people, making her feel terribly uncomfortable. Not to mention, getting him to leave a party before midnight was nearly impossible; he always had to have one more drink.

But Aaron was a completely different man—one who treated her with love and respect—when he was sober. And, thankfully, he wasn't drunk on a regular basis. So Jennifer convinced herself that she could get Aaron to change. She started by trying to tell Aaron that if he really loved her, he would stop drinking. But her tears and pleas got her nowhere. On another occasion, she calmly explained to him how it felt to be in a relationship with someone who drank as he did. She even came up with some similar examples from his life that she thought he might be able to relate to. Still nothing.

One night she tried screaming, cursing, and calling him names; another time, she simply got wasted with him. Neither Aaron's behavior nor his drinking changed. The only thing that changed was Jennifer—the once hopeful young woman was now physically and mentally exhausted. She had taken Aaron's drinking personally, and because of that, her behavior was entirely reactive. He was her Cause; she was his Effect.

Thankfully, Jennifer realized this after countless failed attempts at trying to change him. So, she decided to focus her efforts on someone new—herself. What steps could she take to make her life more joyful? First she started to see that Aaron's drinking had nothing whatsoever to do with her. This was a real turning point. Once she made this distinction, she was able to approach Aaron with compassion—instead of the anger and resentment she had felt before. By letting go of her expectations of how Aaron *should* be, she was able to see that nothing she could do would free him from his personal pain and obstacles. He was in charge of his life, just as she was in charge of hers. Eventually Jennifer broke up with Aaron, but the lessons she learned from this relationship will remain with her.

While it's true that we cannot take another person's pain away, we can by all means serve as a living example. We can try our best to be a role model and a beacon of Light. By doing so, we draw others to the wisdom of Kabbalah. In fact, this is the most effective way to teach Kabbalah. There's no need to convince someone of the invaluable worth of this wisdom. It speaks for itself. No preaching required.

That is how I learned—from role models like my mother and father who imparted their knowledge with a gentle patience that left me wanting to find out more. Each and every day of my life,

I am reminded of their great kindness. And around every corner, their goodness is reflected back to me. During times when they desperately needed help from others, they offered their help instead.

Now my parents aren't superheroes or ordained saints. They don't live lives free of struggle or frustration. And they experience pain as deeply as you or I. But despite their obstacles, they have always managed to bring certainty into everything they do. The establishment of The Kabbalah Centre is a testament to this, as is their relationship with one another.

My mother and father didn't come into this world with extraordinary amounts of patience, endurance, and compassion. Not at all. They had to work for these traits before they could put them to use helping others. They did this by facing their obstacles, grounding themselves in certainty, utilizing the power of the Hebrew letters, and removing their egos from the equation. Easier said than done, but they did it (and continue to do it) every day of their lives. That's the power of Kabbalah.

And it doesn't end with my parents, or with you or with me. How we choose to live our lives affects every single person on this planet. That means every time we act proactively and share our love with others, we are making a global impact. In fact, the state of the world is merely the sum total of all of the interactions of humanity. Black holes in space, global warming, school shootings, unwanted pregnancies, peace treaties, suicide bombers, available parking spots: everything depends on the interactions between one human being and another.

When the ancient sages declared that the Earth was the center of the universe, they were not referring to its position on a map of the cosmos. They were speaking in spiritual terms. Our spiritual actions, be they reactive or proactive, drive the universe. The simple reactive act of bad-mouthing a friend, yelling at your little brother, or copying test answers from a classmate tilts the entire planet towards darkness and away from Light. This is the responsibility we carry. Some might see it as a burden; I call it a gift.

That's because within this awesome responsibility exists the potential for tilting our entire world toward the Light of the Creator. Every time we reel in our ego by admitting jealousy, every time we let go of our long-held opinions, every time we resist the urge to seek status and approval—each and every act of Resistance—makes an enormous difference in the earth's spiritual balance.

The Opponent, of course, would prefer us to remain perpetually lop-sided in his favor. To this end, he will do his best to talk you out of the spiritual truths outlined in this book. *We have no control,* he'll say convincingly. *We are but leaves blowing in the wind, and only the lucky will survive the journey.* But we know now that there is no such thing as "lucky" and "unlucky." And we do have control—over our self-destructive thoughts, behaviors, reactions, and lives.

Having all this control is not *easy*, but it is *simple*. There are worlds of difference between these two words. Taking the easy path leads us to Bread of Shame, while the simple path, the one that requires nothing more than honesty and willingness, leads us precisely where we have longed to go for millennia. I'll be the first to tell you that practicing the principles in this book are challenging, as you have probably experienced by now. Trying to live our lives with full accountability is perhaps the most challenging job in the world.

It is so much easier for us to crusade for some new cause, seek out a new path of wisdom, or try to change the world; easier than it is to look inward, and transform ourselves. But that is exactly what is required of us. It's time to say good-bye to playing the victim and to accept responsibility for everything—the good, the bad, and the ugly—that happens in our lives.

If you have made it this far on the journey, you are more than up for the challenge. But if you should ever feel like you are in danger of losing your foothold, pick up this book and read it again. Start a fresh journal while you are at it and work through the exercises one more time. Our lives are in constant flux, and each day we are learning new and important lessons that are equipping us to move forward along our spiritual path. In the same way, every time you read this book you'll uncover insights you missed the first time around but that are particularly relevant to your life today.

So let go of any expectation of ever arriving at some specific destination; this journey is guaranteed to take a lifetime—a lifetime of incredible opportunities for joy, fulfillment, companionship, love, and laughter. With the Light of the Creator on your side, life becomes one endless tray of delectable desserts. These mouth-watering moments are yours for the taking. Are you prepared to experience such sweetness? You were born ready.

- The traits that frustrate us the most in others are inevitably traits that we possess ourselves.

- Judging ourselves and others is a reactive behavior. Just as there is no need to criticize others for their behavior, we shouldn't judge and berate ourselves for ours.

- Transformation begins when we gently observe our reactive traits.

- You cannot change another human being. It's hard enough to change yourself! And even if you could, you would only bring them Bread of Shame. They must make the change themselves.

- What we can do is provide help on a physical, mental, emotional, or spiritual level and act as positive role models.

- There's no need to convince someone of the invaluable worth of Kabbalah. It speaks for itself.

- Everything is interconnected. Every decision we make tilts the balance of the planet either toward or away from the Light.

- The path of Kabbalah is simple, but it is not always easy, nor should it be.

**exercise:** Have some fun with this one. Make a long list of all the traits in others you find annoying, selfish, or downright wrong! Go into detail. Describe specific situations or encounters. What in particular about these actions really got under your skin? Don't hold back. Make note of how you felt to be on the receiving end of these actions. Now, let's turn this around. Be honest: How many of these traits do you also possess? What steps can you take to correct, or transform, them?

So now it's time to go out there and put these tools to the test by seeing if they make a difference in your life. After all, that's the only test that really matters. Be the cause in your life rather than the effect. Take full responsibility. Make the most of that moment just before you act; use it to move yourself, moment by moment, away from pleasures that disappear in a flash, leaving nothing behind, and toward the rich fulfillment that lasts a lifetime. Don't be deterred by the loud voice inside you that offers up doubts and fears; that's your ego. Do tune in to the quiet, intuitive place inside yourself that lets you know if it feels right. Use the Transformation Formula. Embrace obstacles, for they are your best opportunities for growth. Look for patterns in your behavior, places where you habitually respond in a certain way; these are clues that your life's work lies in replacing that knee-jerk response. Look for traits in others that bother you the most; these are aspects of yourself that you need to acknowledge and transform. Just try these tools out, and see what happens. If you'd like to let me know how it goes, drop me an email at yehuda@kabbalah.com.

I wish you a fun-filled and blessed journey. May your life be filled with Light. May you discover—and share—more joy than you could possibly imagine, and may the challenges you encounter be ones that only add to the infinite fulfillment that is yours to be had.

exercise:

# More Books by Yehuda Berg

### The Power of Kabbalah

Imagine your life filled with unending joy, purpose, and contentment. Imagine your days infused with pure insight and energy. This is *The Power of Kabbalah*. It is the path from the momentary pleasure that most of us settle for, to the lasting fulfillment that is yours to claim. Your deepest desires are waiting to be realized. Find out how, in this basic introduction to the ancient wisdom of Kabbalah.

### Also available: *The Power of Kabbalah Card Deck*

### The 72 Names of God: Technology for the Soul™

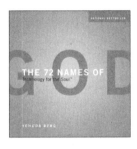

The 72 Names of God are not "names" in any ordinary sense, but a state-of-the-art technology that deeply touches the human soul and is the key to ridding yourself of depression, stress, stagnation, anger, and many other emotional and physical problems. The Names represent a connection to the infinite spiritual current that flows through the universe. When you correctly bring these power sources together, you are able to gain control over your life and transform it for the better.

### Living Kabbalah: A Practical System for Making the Power Work for You

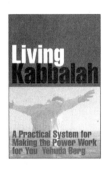

*Living Kabbalah* is a unique system of technology meant for you to use to transform your life and achieve true and lasting fulfillment. In these pages, you will find practical tools and exercises to help you break negative patterns, overcome challenges, and incorporate the time-tested wisdom of Kabbalah into your daily life. Noted author and teacher Yehuda Berg provides a clear blueprint that guides you step-by-step along the path toward the ultimate attainment of all that you need and desire.

Tap into a greater power—the power of Kabbalah—and learn to live more fully, richly, and joyfully every day, starting today!

### Rebooting: Defeating Depression with the Power of Kabbalah

An estimated 18 million people in the United States suffer from depression—that's almost 10% of the population. So chances are good that you have, or someone you know has, been affected by it. Antidepressants, counseling, herbal remedies—all have been known to help treat the symptoms, but sometimes they fall short. If only you could click on the "Restart" button and get your internal software back on track. Now, in *Rebooting*, noted kabbalistic scholar and author Yehuda Berg shows how you can do just that by reconnecting with desire and light to emerge from this debilitating darkness.

### The Spiritual Rules of Engagement

If you've been searching for your soul mate without success, maybe it's time to try a new approach: *The Spiritual Rules of Engagement*. Kabbalah teaches that we are not alone, and that we are destined to be happy. Find out how the Laws of the Universe work in your favor, once you begin to understand them and recognize the full potential for true love and sharing that lies within all of us. If you are willing to make the spiritual effort, you will see that real connection, both with the Light and with another human being, comes down to a matter of consciousness and certainty. The power is in your hands.

# Technology for the Soul™ Series

### Kabbalah on Love

This charming little book has a simple yet profound message: Love is not something you learn or acquire but an essence within, waiting to be revealed. Buried by layers of ego, fear, shame, doubt, low self-esteem, and other limitations, the incredibly powerful force that is love can only be activated by sharing and serving unconditionally. Only then will the layers fall away and the essence of love reveal itself. The book draws the distinction between love and need, which is a selfish product of ego, and reminds us that we cannot love someone else until we figure out how to love ourselves and connect with the love within.

### Beyond Blame: A Full-Responsibility Approach to Life

If you think that chaos and suffering in your life is random or caused by external circumstances, think again! It's time to take personal responsibility for life's problems rather than give in to the tendency to blame others for them. In this book, you'll find simple, practical tools to help you overcome this negative tendency and live a happier, more productive life. Learn how to eliminate "victim consciousness" and improve your life, starting today.

## Kabbalah on Pain: How to Use It to Lose It

Learn how to use your emotional pain to your advantage and how to release its grip on you forever. When you avoid, ignore, or bury your pain, you only prolong psychic agony. But Kabbalah teaches a method for detaching from the source of this pain—human ego—and thereby forcing ego to take on and deal with your pain. When you choose the path of the soul where only ego suffers, you will begin to move toward the state of pure joy that is your destiny.

## The Monster is Real: How to Face Your Fears and Eliminate Them Forever

Admit it—at this very moment, you're afraid of something, or maybe even lots of things. This book shows you how to attack and defeat your fears at their most basic level. It offers practical kabbalistic tools for eliminating fear at its source so you can begin to live life to its fullest extent.

### The Red String Book: The Power of Protection

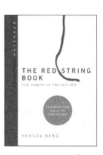

Discover the ancient wisdom behind the popularity of the Red String—the timeless technology known as Kabbalah. Worn on the left wrist, an authentic Red String provides protection against the "Evil Eye"—all negative effects that exist in the world. In *The Red String Book*, Yehuda Berg reveals how everyone can learn to use this simple yet effective tool for self-defense and healing.

### God Does Not Create Miracles, You Do!

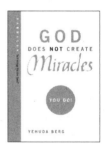

Stop waiting for a miracle and start making miracles happen! Discover powerful tools to help you break free of whatever is standing between you and the complete happiness you deserve. This book gives you the formula for creating the connection with the true source of miracles that lies only within yourself.

### The Dreams Book: Finding Your Way in the Dark

Lift the curtain of reality and discover the secrets of dream interpretation that have remained hidden for centuries. Learn powerful techniques to attract soul mates, improve relationships, recognize career opportunities, and much more. This book holds the key to navigating the dreamscape, where the answers to life's questions are revealed.

## Kabbalah on Green: Consciousness and The Environment

Green is a powerful color according to the ancient wisdom of Kabbalah, because it is the color of the Central Column that stands between right and left, positive and negative, giving and receiving. As such, it represents the balance that is so important to the survival of our planet. Green is also the color of healing, both of the soul and of the Earth. Kabbalah teaches that eco-consciousness and higher consciousness are inextricably linked. In this incisive and thought-provoking book, Yehuda Berg reveals the importance of this relationship; and he explains why the forces of environmental destruction can only be overcome by each and every individual's personal transformation, before "green" can be achieved on a global scale.

# More Books to Help Bring the Wisdom of Kabbalah into Your Life

### *Nano: Technology of Mind over Matter*
### By Rav Berg

Kabbalah is all about attaining control over the physical world, including our personal lives, at the most fundamental level of reality. It's about achieving and extending mind over matter and developing the ability to create fulfillment, joy, and happiness by controlling everything at the most basic level of existence. In this way, Kabbalah predates and presages the most exciting trend in recent scientific and technological development, the application of nanotechnology to all areas of life in order to create better, stronger, and more efficient results.

### *The Secret: Unlocking the Source of Joy & Fulfillment*
### By Michael Berg

*The Secret* reveals the essence of life in its most concise and powerful form. Several years before the latest "Secret" phenomenon, Michael Berg shared the amazing truths of the world's oldest spiritual wisdom in this book. In it, he has pieced together an ancient puzzle to show that our common understanding of life's purpose is actually backwards, and that anything less than complete joy and fulfillment can be changed by correcting this misperception.

## Kabbalistic Astrology: And the Meaning of Our Lives
## By Rav Berg

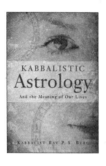

Discover your true nature and destiny, and how to shape it, through the power of Kabbalistic astrology.

Much more than a book of horoscopes, *Kabbalistic Astrology* is a tool for understanding one's individual nature at its deepest level and putting that knowledge to immediate use in the real world. It explains why destiny is not the same as predestination; it teaches that we have many possible futures and can become masters of our fate.

## Secrets of the Zohar: Stories and Meditations to Awaken the Heart
## By Michael Berg

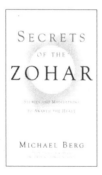

The *Zohar*'s secrets are the secrets of the Bible, passed on as oral tradition and then recorded as a sacred text that remained hidden for thousands of years. They have never been revealed quite as they are here in these pages, which decipher the codes behind the best stories of the ancient sages and offer a special meditation for each one. Entire portions of the *Zohar* are presented, with the Aramaic and its English translation in side-by-side columns. This allows you to scan and to read aloud so that you can draw on the *Zohar*'s full energy and achieve spiritual transformation. Open this book and open your heart to the Light of the *Zohar*!

# The Kabbalah Centre®

## What is Kabbalah?

Kabbalah is the world's oldest body of spiritual wisdom, containing the long-hidden keys to the secrets of the Universe, as well as the keys to the mysteries of the human heart and soul. It's a workable system that allows you to understand your purpose for being here experiencing the joy you were put on Earth to have. In fact, that's what Kabbalah means to receive, to get.

Kabbalah teaches that in order to claim the gifts you were created to receive, you need to earn them by undertaking your spiritual work the process of fundamentally transforming yourself as you climb out of the darkness and into the Light. By helping you recognize the sources of negativity in your own mind and heart, Kabbalah gives you the tools for positive change.

Kabbalistic teachings explain the complexities of the material and the nonmaterial Universe and the physical and metaphysical nature of all humankind.

Moses, Pythagoras, and Sir Isaac Newton are a few of the individuals who studied Kabbalah to understand the spiritual laws of the Universe and their effect on the physical world.

Kabbalah is meant to be used, not merely learned. It can help you remove chaos, pain, and suffering from your life and bring you clarity, understanding, and freedom.

## Who Can Study?

Today, millions of people of all faiths have discovered the wisdom and experienced the powerful effects of studying Kabbalah.

Why shouldn't they? Kabbalah works. When the wisdom and practical tools of Kabbalah are applied in life, positive experiences are the result. And Kabbalah can enhance the practice of any religion.

## What Is The Kabbalah Centre®?

The Kabbalah Centre® is a spiritual and educational organization dedicated to bringing the wisdom of Kabbalah to the world. The Centre itself has existed for more than 80 years, but its spiritual lineage extends back to Rav Isaac Luria in the 16th century and even further back to Rav Shimon bar Yochai, who revealed the principal text of Kabbalah, the *Zohar*, more than 2,000 years ago.

The Kabbalah Centre® was founded in 1922 by Rav Yehuda Ashlag, one of the greatest kabbalists of the 20th Century. When Rav Ashlag left this world, leadership of The Centre was taken on by Rav Yehuda Brandwein. Before his passing, Rav Brandwein designated Rav Berg as director of The Kabbalah Centre®. Now, for more than 30 years, The Centre has been under the direction of Rav Berg, his wife Karen Berg, and their sons, Yehuda Berg and Michael Berg.

Although there are many scholarly studies of Kabbalah, The Kabbalah Centre® does not teach Kabbalah as an academic discipline but as a way of creating a better life. The mission of The Kabbalah Centre® is to make the practical tools and spiritual teachings of Kabbalah available and accessible to everyone regardless of religion, ethnicity, gender, or age.

The Kabbalah Centre® makes no promises. But if people are willing to work hard to grow and become actively sharing, caring, and tolerant human beings, Kabbalah teaches that they will then experience fulfillment and joy in a way previously unknown to them. This sense of fulfillment, however, comes gradually and is always the result of the student's spiritual work.

Our ultimate goal is for all humanity to gain the happiness and fulfillment that is our true destiny.

Kabbalah teaches its students to question and test everything they learn. One of the most important teachings of Kabbalah is that there is no coercion in spirituality.

## What Does The Kabbalah Centre® Offer?

Local Kabbalah Centres around the world offer onsite lectures, classes, study groups, holiday celebrations, and a community of teachers and fellow students. To find a Centre near you, go to www.kabbalah.com.

For those of you unable to access a physical Kabbalah Centre due to the constraints of location or time, we have other ways to participate in The Kabbalah Centre® community.

At www.kabbalah.com, we feature online blogs, newsletters, weekly wisdom, a store, and much more.

It's a wonderful way to stay tuned in and in touch, and it gives you access to programs that will expand your mind and challenge you to continue your spiritual work.

## Student Support

The Kabbalah Centre® empowers people to take responsibility for their own lives. It's about the teachings, not the teachers. But on your journey to personal growth, things can be unclear and sometimes rocky, so it is helpful to have a coach or teacher.

All Student Support instructors have studied Kabbalah under the direct supervision of Kabbalist Rav Berg, widely recognized as the preeminent kabbalist of our time.

We have also created opportunities for you to interact with other Student Support students through study groups, monthly connections, holiday retreats, and other events held around the country.

notes:

notes:

notes:

notes: